BRITAIN

1815–1851

Queen Victoria and Prince Albert arriving at the opening of the Great Exhibition, May 1st 1851

Longman History Studies in Depth

BRITAIN
1815-1851

R. A. Rees

Longman

To Vicky

Longman Group UK Limited
Longman House, Burnt Mill, Harlow, Essex, CM20 2JE, England and
Associated Companies throughout the World.

© Longman Group UK Limited 1990

First published 1990
ISBN 0 582 332184

Set in 10/11 point Palatino, Linotron 202
Printed in Great Britain by Bell and Bain LTD, Glasgow.

British Library Cataloguing in Publication Data
Rees, R. A.
    Britain 1815–51. – (Longman history studies in depth).
    1. Great Britain. 1760–1830
    I. Title
    941.073

ISBN 0–582–33218–4

CONTENTS

Acknowledgements

We are grateful to the following for permission to reproduce photographs. City of Bradford Metropolitan Council/Central Library page 54; Birmingham Museum and Art Gallery, page 114 (right); City of Bristol Museum and Art Gallery, page 24; Courtesy of the Trustees of the British Museum, page 26; By permission of the Syndics of Cambridge University Library, page 30, 140; Dudley Public Libraries, page 61; Fotomas Index, pages 14, 86; GWR Museum, Swindon, page 131; These items are included by permission of the County Archivist, Hertfordshire Record Office, pages 16 (left), 16 (above right), 16 (below), 17 (above), 17 (below); The Hulton Picture Company, pages 8, 19, 20, 23, 32 (above), 37 (left), 37 (right), 40, 50, 67, 68, 77, 81, 82 , 83, 84, 85, 87, 104, 106, 115, 119, 121; ILN Picture Library pages 32 (below), 38, 43, 58, 95, 109, 126, 137; Ironbridge Gorge Museum Trust/Elton Collection pages 42, 75, 134, 138, 139; Kirklees Library and Art Galley, page 70; the Mansell Collection, pages 9 (below), 10, 11, 15, 34, 35, 45 (above), 59, 74, 79, 90, 91, 92, 98, 111, 113, 123, 125, 128 (above), 136 (below), 141; Mary Evans Picture Library, pages 12, 39, 62, 66, 89, 96, 108, 133; The Mitchell Library, Glasgow, page 114 (left); Trustees of the National Library of Scotland, page 101 (right); 'Board of Trustees of the National Museums and Galleries on Merseyside' (Walker Art Gallery, Liverpool) page 9 (above); National Museum of Wales, pages 76, 78; National Railway Museum, York, page 132; Norfolk Record Office, (PD 78/91 + C/GP 1/519) pages 45 (below), 52; Public Record Office, London, (H0107/2309) Crown Copyright; Reproduced by Permission, page 65; Reproduced by permission of *Punch*, pages 47 (right), 110 (left), (below right), 142; Trustees of the Science Museum London, pages 117, 118, 128 (below), 129; Taken from E.B. Hamel's "Illustrations of Tamworth", 1829 © Tamworth Borough Council, page 94; West Yorkshire, Archive Service, Bradford: Bradford County Borough building plan, page 63. The following material has been taken from: 'CAPTAIN SWING', Lawrence and Wishart, 1969, pages 47 (left), 48; 'The State of The Poor' by F.M. Eden, 1797, page 46; 'Britain Since 1700', by R.S. Cootes, Longman 1968, page 101 (left); 'A Social and Economic History of Industrial Britain', by J. Robottom, Longman 1986, page 28; Then and There Series: 'Edwin Chadwick, Poor Law and Public Health', by R. Watson, Longman 1969, page 51 (above), (below); Then and There Series: 'Sailing Ships and Emigrants in Victorian Times', by A. Grant, Longman 1972, page 110 (above right).

Cover: Painting by Carmichael: High Level Bridge at Newcastle, 1849 'Reproduced by kind permission of the University of Newcastle upon Tyne'.

Picture Research by Sandie Huskinson-Rolfe (Photoseekers)

Details of source material are given after each extract. If several extracts are taken from the same source, full details appear after the first extract. Where extracts are quoted within the narrative, additional details are given below:

p. 15 Robert Southey, *Letters from England*, 1807; p. 22 *Leeds Mercury*, 27.7.1830; p. 38 Benjamin Disraeli, *Sybil*, Book 2 Chapter v; p. 39 John Burnett, *Useful Toil*, Allen Lane, 1974; p. 40 Anna Maria Fay, *Victorian Days in England: Letters of an American Girl 1851–2*, Boston and New York, 1923; p. 41 quoted in C. Woodham Smith, *Florence Nightingale*, Constable, 1950; p. 50 *Poor Law Amendment Act*, 1834; p. 67 *Parliamentary Papers*, 1842, vol. 27; p. 87 Select Committee on Secondary Punishments, *Parliamentary Papers*, 1831–2, vii; p. 87 *Parliamentary Papers*, 1847, vol. 12; p. 111 A Joyce, *A Homestead History*, Melbourne, 1942; p. 112 A.G.L. Shaw, *The Story of Australia*, Faber, 1955; p. 112 and 113 J. Prebble, *The Highland Clearances*, Penguin, 1963; p. 121 S. Smiles, *Story of the Life of George Stephenson*, Murray, 1862; p. 119 J. Francis, *A History of the English Railway*, Longman, 1851; p. 124 J. Francis, *op. cit.*; p. 130 *ibid.*; p. 129 and 130 T. Coleman, *The Railway Navvies*, Hutchinson, 1965; p. 134 quoted in G.R. Hawke, *Railways and Economic Growth in England and Wales 1840–1970*, OUP, 1970; p. 137 from *Principal Speeches and Addresses of HRH the Prince Consort*, 1862; p. 141 *Illustrated London News*, 28 June, 1851.

To the reader

Weights and Measures

The people who lived in Britain between 1815 and 1851 used a system of weights and measures which was different from the one we use today. This book is about Britain at that time, and so all the weights and measures are given in the old, Imperial system. The table below can be used if you need to convert any measurements into the modern metric system.

	Imperial Measures	*Metric equivalent*
Length	1 inch (1 in)	2.5 cms
	12 inches (1 foot)	30.0 cms
	3 feet (1 yard)	1.0 m
	1760 yards (1 mile)	1.6 km
Weight	1 ounce (1 oz)	28.00 grams
	16 ozs (1 pound 11b)	.45 kg
	1121 lbs (1 hundred weight 1 cwt)	50.00 kg
	20 cwts (1 ton)	1 tonne
Capacity	1 pint (1 pt)	.56 litres
	8 pints (1 gallon)	4.50 litres

Money

The system of money used in Britain at that time was different, too. Remember, though, that it is not particularly sensible to change the old system into our decimal one, because the value of money has altered a great deal.

2 farthings	=	1 halfpenny ($\frac{1}{2}$d)
4 farthings	=	1 penny (1d)
12 pennies	=	1 shilling (1/-)
20 shillings	=	1 pound (£1)

INTRODUCTION

Britain in 1815

By 1815 Britain had, with one short break, been at war for twenty-two years. The French Emperor, Napoleon I, had tried to rule most of Europe. Many military alliances had been formed between different European countries to fight Napoleon. Land battles had been fought in countries as far apart as Russia and Spain; sea battles as far distant as the waters off Copenhagen and the mouth of the river Nile. None of these had succeeded in defeating him for ever. Finally, on 18th June 1815, British and Prussian armies were victorious at the Battle of Waterloo. Napoleon was forced to give up his throne four days later.

Britain was left as the strongest and most powerful country in the world. The British colonial empire was larger and more widespread than that of any other country; Britain had the largest navy in the world, and more merchant ships than any other country; these merchant sailing ships carried more of the world's trade than the ships of any other country. London was the biggest city and financial centre of the world.

One of the reasons for this was that British industry was the most developed in the world. The oldest industry of all, agriculture, was changing slowly and steadily to produce more food and greater quantities of raw materials like wool. The great open fields, which were mainly in the midlands and the south of Britain, had been replaced by smaller fields surrounded by hedges, walls and fences. These enclosures meant that stock-breeding could be improved and new crops tried out. More food was produced, as well as greater quantities of raw materials such as wool. One of the best ways of spreading the new ideas about farming was at fairs and festivals like the sheep-shearing festival held on the Duke of Woburn's estate which is shown below.

In the eighteenth century people used the word 'manufacture' (which comes from Latin words meaning 'make by hand') to describe the way in which hundreds of goods, from woollen cloth to iron nails, were made in Great Britain. Manpower was the basic, and cheapest, source of power used in manufacturing. The driving force of all looms, forges and mines was provided by the men and women who worked them.

'Woburn Sheep-shearing' painted by G. Garrard, 1804

'A pit-head', 1820

Factory children, the West Riding of Yorkshire, 1814

'The Harvest' from Pyne's Microcosm, published 1804

Leeds in 1815

Gradually water power and then, later, steam power became the main driving force of British industry.

The pit-head scene on page 9, which was painted anonymously about 1820, shows the use of steam-powered pumping engines and winding gear in a coal-mine. The development of machines powered by water meant, for example, that large numbers of people could work together in one building to produce cloth quickly and economically. The use of water and steam power meant that the production of raw materials such as coal, iron and cotton increased dramatically. These could be used to supply other industries and trades which themselves expanded and prospered.

Transport in 1815 was by road or canal. Road transport was faster, but canals were cheaper. It was usual for heavy goods and raw materials to be moved by canal barge wherever possible. 3,000 miles of canals carried non-perishable goods from mines, quarries and manufacturing regions to cities and ports. The 2,000 miles of roads looked after by Turnpike Trusts meant that fast and regular mail and passenger horse-drawn coach services were possible between major towns. Many roads, however, were little more than cart-tracks which turned to mud and became impassable in bad weather. News – good or bad – could only travel as fast as a galloping horse.

In 1815 about one third of all the people living in Great Britain made their living from agriculture. Towns and cities, however, were growing rapidly. Not only was the population increasing, but men, women and children were moving in from the countryside to industrial cities such as Nottingham, Birmingham, Manchester and Leeds.

Great Britain, in 1815, was the richest country in the world. It was also a country of enormous contrasts. William Howitt, who was a popular author and journalist, described as late as 1838 a rich man's house – the plate and porcelain, the cellars and kitchens, library, dining rooms, breakfast rooms and drawing rooms – and then went on to describe a labourer's one-roomed, mud-floored cottage. 'We must certainly think', Howitt wrote, 'that one has too much for the insurance of comfort, or the other must have extremely too little.'

From a total population (England, Wales and Scotland) of around 13,000,000 people, only 500,000 were allowed to vote in general elections. None of these electors were women. The right to vote was closely connected with the ownership of land and property. No-one was allowed to combine with other workers to form a trades union, and education was, in the main, left to parents to decide whether or not they could afford it for their children. The old, the sick and the ill who could not work to earn money and who had no families to care for them had to ask their local parish for help. So did those who could not find jobs. In 1815 just over £6,000,000 was spent by the better-off people in providing food, clothing and shelter for paupers. Most people took it for granted that people were born to wealth or poverty, and that there was little anyone could, or should, do to alter matters.

Change was, however, to come. In this book you will read about the enormous changes which happened in Great Britain between 1815 and 1851. These changes affected the lives of almost everybody from crossing-sweepers to doctors, from washerwomen to duchesses, from beggars to government ministers.

1

THE VOTE

The Parliamentary System before 1832

The Triple Cord

Edmund Burke was an important Member of Parliament in the eighteenth century. In 1796, a year before he died, he wrote a letter in which he described the way in which Great Britain had been governed in the eighteenth century. This is part of what he said:

> 'The King, and his faithful subjects, the lords and commons of this realm, – one triple cord which no man can break.'

It was this 'triple cord' which was seen by Burke, and those who thought like him, as being the great strength of the British system. The monarch, the members of the House of Commons and the members of the House of Lords all played different, but equally important, parts in the government of Great Britain. In the eighteenth and early nineteenth centuries, governments were concerned with matters such as raising taxes, dealing with disorder, maintaining the army and navy, conducting foreign policy and fighting wars. It was not the job of government to become involved in providing education or health services, or to deal with matters such as housing, poverty or unemployment.

The king appointed the ministers of state. In this way the king was sure to have a major influence on government policies. Parliament, however, controlled the finances. Money was needed to put any policy into action. This meant that the king's policies could not be carried out unless his ministers had the support of Parliament, because it was Parliament who would vote them the money they wanted. In particular, ministers needed the support of the House of Commons, because it was the Commons, and not the Lords, who were allowed to introduce financial measures. The king was able to control a section of the Commons because well over a hundred Members of Parliament (MPs) were de-

William Pitt, who was Prime Minister 1783–1801, speaking to the House of Commons in 1793

pendent upon him and his government for their seats and incomes from jobs as, for example, Court officers, civil servants and army and navy officers receiving government pensions, and so they tended to vote for the king's policies. These MPs were often called 'placemen'. However, the number of placemen was not sufficient for the king to be sure that the Commons would support his policies and his ministers all the time. Therefore, the king could not insist that his ministers carry out policies which were opposed by the Commons. Neither, however, could the Commons insist that the king appoint ministers whom they liked and whom he disliked. There had to be a balance.

The House of Lords played an important part in the government of Great Britain. Most government ministers sat in the Lords, as did leaders of the army, civil service and the Church of England. Most of the great landowners were peers, and sat in the House of Lords. Not only did they own vast estates, but many controlled areas (constituencies) which sent MPs to the House of Commons. An historian, Sir Lewis Namier, calculated that in the election of 1761, about 111 MPs owed their seats to the direct influence of about fifty-five peers. Even so, this was not enough to guarantee that the Commons would always support the Lords and the king's ministers. Neither was it enough to guarantee that the measures proposed by the Commons would always be supported by the Lords. It was quite usual for the House of Lords to join with the king in opposing a measure which had been passed by the House of Commons.

The House of Commons consisted of 658 MPs, all of whom were elected in some way or other. Electors did not vote for a political party or for a national programme. They usually voted on personal and local, rather than national, issues. There were no nationally organised parties with published election manifestos. Indeed, there were no formal political parties at all. There were groups of MPs called 'Whigs' and 'Tories', but these were usually made up of politicians who organised themselves into groups based on family and friends, or on a very general sharing of ideas and attitudes. An MP might vote with the Whigs on one occasion and with the Tories on another. This would be considered entirely proper. Placemen, however, almost always voted with the government.

The vast majority of MPs in the eighteenth century, however, were independent members who could afford to spend time doing this unpaid job of work at Westminster because they believed it was important. They were not bound to ministers and the government by the need for an income, and they were not necessarily bound to either the Whigs or to the Tories by ties of family. No government could be certain of the support of all of these independent MPs, or even of a large proportion of them. Yet all governments needed their support if they were to survive for long.

This intricate system of checks and balances shifted and changed throughout the eighteenth century. However, the three elements considered vital to effective government – the Crown, the Commons and the Lords – remained almost equal partners in power.

Constituencies: Counties and Boroughs

The part of the country which a Member of Parliament represented was, and still is, called a constituency. There were two different kinds of constituency: county and borough. Each county in England and Wales, no matter how small or large, nor how many people lived there, was allowed to have two MPs. Most Scottish counties had one MP.

Many counties contained towns which, because they had been important ports or markets, had in the past been made 'parliamentary boroughs'. This meant that they, like the counties, could send two representatives to Parliament. In Scotland, the burghs were grouped in fours, with each group being entitled to one MP.

Dunwich had been a bustling Suffolk port in the thirteenth century, when it was granted the status of 'borough'. By 1831, however, with only forty-four houses, it had clearly lost its early importance. Yet it was still entitled to borough status, and to two MPs. Similarly, six Cornish boroughs, with hardly 1,000 inhabitants each, were entitled to send, between them, twelve representatives to Parliament. Boroughs like this were called 'rotten boroughs'. Many of the early boroughs had been created in the six southern counties which bordered the English Channel. In 1801, one third of England's MPs came from these counties, yet only 15 per cent of the population of England lived there. Most of the counties and boroughs which sent representatives to Parliament were in the south and west of England.

In contrast, large northern towns, such as Manchester with 182,000 inhabitants in 1831, Leeds with 123,000 inhabitants and midland towns like Birmingham with 144,000 inhabitants, did not have a single representative in the House of Commons. This was because in mediaeval times, when boroughs were first created, towns like these were unimportant small villages which did not merit borough status and their own MP.

The Franchise: the Voters

Sir Philip Francis, writing about his election in 1802 as MP for Appleby, said:

'. . . The fact is that yesterday morning between 11 and 12 I was unanimously elected by one Elector, to represent this Ancient Borough in Parliament . . .'

The right to vote went with certain qualifications which were mostly to do with ownership of land. Whether or not a man was allowed to vote in a parliamentary election depended upon where he lived and what he owned. If he lived in a county, and owned freehold land or property which was worth at least £2 a year, then he had the right to vote. If he lived in a borough, the situation was more complicated. Whether or not he had the vote depended upon the ancient rights and customs of that borough. In some boroughs, 'burgage' boroughs, voting rights were handed down from father to son; in others, it was enough to own a hearth and not claim money from the poor-rate. These were known as 'potwalloper' boroughs. In many boroughs only members of the local town corporation were entitled to vote. 'Scot and lot' boroughs, on the other hand, allowed all men who paid certain ancient taxes the right to vote. All this meant that, in some boroughs, nearly all the adult men could vote; in others, only one man in a hundred could vote.

Throughout the whole country, the actual number of people who could vote was, in fact, very small. In 1831, out of a population of 24 million people, less than half a million were entitled to vote. None of these were women.

Elections

The law said that there had to be a general election at least every seven years. However, in constituencies where there were the same number of candidates as there were seats, there was no point in holding an actual election. Indeed, in the hundred years before 1832, no more than eleven county seats and eighty-two borough seats were actually contested in a general election. If a landowner supported a candidate, there was often no point in anyone else trying to get elected to that seat. Indeed, in the 'pocket boroughs', where one landowner owned enough property to be able to control the election, no one would dare to oppose him or the candidate he had chosen.

Elections, when they did happen, were usually very lively affairs! The polls were open for several days. In this way everyone who was qualified to vote had the opportunity to do so. Some might have long journeys from the surrounding countryside into the nearest town. The candidates paid for the cost of transporting the electors, and for the board and lodging of those they thought were going to vote for them. A successful candidate (or candidates) usually had to pay for vast banquets and other sorts of celebrations as well. Candidates had to have a private income since they would not be paid a salary whilst they were MPs.

There were many ways of persuading the electors to vote for a certain candidate. Some were not at all

This picture, called 'Election Dinner', was painted by William Hogarth in 1754. Hogarth (1697–1764) became famous for his paintings and engravings which told a moral story. He often exaggerated people's expressions and actions in order to emphasise the point he was trying to make. Look carefully at this picture and try to decide what Hogarth was saying about the whole business of candidates giving treats to their supporters at election time

straightforward, as Robert Southey described in 1807:

> 'Some seats are private property; the right of voting belongs to a few householders . . . and these are votes commanded by the owner of the estate. The fewer they are, the more easily they are managed . . . Where the number of voters is greater . . . the business is more difficult and expensive. The candidate must deal individually with the constituents, who sell themselves to the highest bidder . . . At Aylesbury a bowl of guineas stood in the committee room, and the voters were helped [*given money*] out of it. The price of votes varies according to their number. In some places it is as low as forty shillings (£2) in others it is thirty pounds.'

Sometimes money was promised which could not be paid. This account is taken from a radical pamphlet, *The Extraordinary Blue Book*, written in 1831 by people who wanted to change the electoral system:

> 'At Hull, one of the sitting members dared not appear before his constituents – not for any defalcation [*fault*] of duty in Parliament, but because he had not paid the "polling money" from the last election.'

Voting

The vote was not secret. Each voter had to walk onto a platform, called the hustings, and say out loud the name of the man for whom he was voting. This was then written down by the poll clerk, who gave the voter a certificate. This certificate meant that the voter could claim back, from the candidate, any money he had had to spend in getting himself to the poll. The voters were then told, usually by posters which were put up in all the towns and villages, where and when they could claim the money that was due to them.

Many voters elected the candidate their landlord supported; a large number voted for the candidate who paid them the most money to do so. Many candidates spent a great deal of money in bribes and 'treats' to make sure that they got themselves elected to the House of Commons.

This picture is the third picture in Hogarth's series called 'The Election'. The picture on page 14 is also in this series. This scene is called 'The Polling' and shows candidates bringing in all sorts of people to vote for them. What kind of people does Hogarth show?

SOURCE WORK:
The Old Parliamentary System

The Hertfordshire County Election of 1805

The events surrounding the Hertfordshire county election in 1805, and the way in which the election was run, were typical of elections held in Britain before 1832.

Hertfordshire was a county, and so had two Members of Parliament. The death of one of them, the Hon. Penistone Lamb, led to a by-election. This was held in 1805. There were two candidates, the Hon. Thomas Brand and William Baker.

SOURCE A

This is an election handbill, printed in 1805, to persuade electors to vote for Thomas Brand.

FREEHOLDERS OF HERTS.

BE not deceived by the WORDS of your Candidates. Judge them by their ACTIONS. Know then that Mr. BRAND is the man, who, fucceeding to an Eftate of Eight Thoufand Pounds a Year, went into retirement, and lived on Four Hundred, that he might be enabled to pay his Father's Debts, which he difcharged to a great amount, though he was not obliged to pay one fhilling! During his retirement he has ftudied the Laws of his Country, and the Britifh Conftitution. Thus having fitted himfelf for your Reprefentative, and given the beft fecurity for his INDEPENDENCE, he folicits your Vote; and if you elect him, he will manifeft the fame HONOUR, JUSTICE and LIBERALITY towards the PUBLIC, as have been confpicuous in his private character.

A FRIEND TO HONESTY AND
INDEPENDENCE.

1. Read the handbill (Source A) carefully.
   (a) What does the handbill tell you about Thomas Brand? Make a list.
   (b) Look down your list. Beside each item you have listed, write 'F' if it is a fact, or 'O' if it is an opinion.
   (c) How is the author of the handbill trying to persuade the electors to vote for Thomas Brand?

2. Read the handbill (Source B) carefully.
   (a) What does the handbill say about William Baker?
   (b) What does the handbill say about Thomas Brand?

SOURCE B

This is an election handbill, printed in 1805, to persuade electors to vote for William Baker.

SERIOUS QUESTIONS,
AND
Serious Answers,
For the Consideration of the ELECTORS of the
County of HERTFORD.

QUESTION.

WHO patronized Arthur O'Connor, that Traitor to his King and Country?

Answer.—The Whig Club—his Friends and Companions.

Question.—Did not the Duke of Norfolk, Charles Fox, Sam. Whitbread, and other Heads of the Whig Club, give Arthur O'Connor, on his Trial, at Maidstone, a Character, which, unfortunately, saved him from the Gallows, and enables him, at the present Moment, to conspire with Bonaparte to enslave your Country and destroy your King?

Question.—Who are the Supporters of Mr. Brand at the present Election?

Answer.—The Whig Club.

Electors of the County of Hertford, reflect, and as Friends to your Country, you will give your Votes to WILLIAM BAKER, Esq. your former worthy Representative.

Swinney and Ferrall, Printers, Birmingham.

3. How is the author of the handbill trying to persuade the electors to vote for William Baker?

4. What are the main differences between the two posters?

SOURCE C

This invitation card was issued just before the election to supporters of Thomas Brand.

HITCHIN, *Saturday, 9th February,* 1805.

THE Favour of your Company is requested to Breakfast with *Mr. Brand's* Friends at the SWAN, in *Hitchin,* on Monday at Six o'Clock, and to proceed in a Body to the Election.

THE High Sheriff having fixed to begin the Business at Ten o'Clock, it is intended to set out from Hitchin, a Quarter before Seven precisely, in order to be in the Field in Time.

The Old Parliamentary System

SOURCE D

This is an extract from a letter written by William Baker to his son. It is dated 22nd February 1805.

'. . . The remainder of Saturday could not be passed from Home. It was better employed in making Preparations for Breakfast at Bayford and Hertingfordbury for such of the Freeholders, as coming from the West and North chose to partake of Refreshment, or leave their Horses – In this our Farm was also included, with the Advantage of Beds for many during the Poll . . .

Sunday 10th was employed in writing, receiving and sending Messengers as usual, Carter, C. Smith, Rawlins, and Dorrien etc etc. were to come in with their Party from the West on the next Day (the Day fixed for the Election), and were to be with us or at Hertingfordbury . . . with Dinner for as many as we could Muster after each Day's Poll . . .'

5. What can be learned from Sources C and D about the ways in which Thomas Brand and William Baker prepared for the election?

SOURCE E

At a poll, each elector shouted out the name of the man for whom he was voting. These votes were written in a poll book, which contained the names of everyone who voted, information as to what it was that entitled them to vote at that particular time, and the name of the person for whom they voted. Poll books were later published.

Constituencies (boroughs and counties) were divided up into smaller areas for voting and for counting the votes. These votes were then added together to find out who had been elected MP for the whole constituency. This source is two pages (opposite) from the Poll Book of the Hitchin Hundred, which was an area of Hertfordshire. Key: H = House; L = Land; M = Mill or malting.

6. Poll books tell us for which candidate each elector voted.
   (a) What else can be discovered from poll books?
   (b) How reliable would this information be?

7. William Baker won the election.
   Is there enough evidence in this source work section to explain why?

Situation of Freehold.	Places of Abode.	Quality of Freehd.	Occupiers.	BAKER.	BRAND.
HITCHIN.					
Edward Waller		H M			Br
Smith Churchill		H			Br
Richard Lucas, Cl.		H			Br
John Maddox		H			Br
Samuel Bell		H			Br
John Crouch Priest	Shitlington	L	T. Hardwick		Br
Wm. Lucas, jun.		H	Richard Atkins		Br
Joseph Lucas		H	W. Richardson		Br
James Deacon		H	James Cousins		Br
T. Burton Bedford	Woolwich	H	Rev. L. Burroug.		Br
W. Langford, jun.		H			Br
John Farmer		H	T. Farmer, sen.		Br
William Bedford		H			Br
Thomas Brown		H L			Br
Thomas Everett		H			Br
Daniel Newton		L			Br
James Wrenn		H L			Br
William Beck	Baker Street	L	Richard Barry		Br
Francis Corrie		H			Br
E.H.D. Radcliffe, Es.		H M			Br
James Milton		H	W. Brown		Br
Thomas Jeeves		H L			Br
Thomas Topham		H			Br
Thomas Chapman		H			Br
George Hayes		L			Br
William Chambers		H			Br
J. Darton, Esq.	Temple Dinsley	H M			Br
Thomas Paternoster		H			Br
John Whitney		H L			Br
James Whitney		H L			Br
Robert Crofts		H			Br
George Collison		H L			Br
Thomas Crawley	Offley Grange	L	John Priest		Br
John Hooper	Dunstable	H L	W. Lucas, jun.	Ba	
James Creasey		H			Br
John Tap		H			Br
Reuben Shadwell		H			Br
John Russell		H			Br
John Morgan		H			Br
James Anderson	Preston	H L			Br
Isaac Duncalf		H L			Br
Samuel Negus		H			Br
Josiah Ison		H	Thos. Hibsden		Br
Dur. Rhudde, D.D.	E. Bereholt, Suf.	H	Dan. Times		Br
Robert Jenner	London	P R A H		Ba	
Samuel Bradley		H	Dan. Field		Br
J. M. Pierson		H		Ba	
Isaac Sharpless		H		Ba	
Charles Nash		H	W. Goodship		Br
John Reed		H			Br
Daniel Nash		H			Br
Thomas Wilshire		H L			Br
Owen Gallaher		H L	Self et al.		Br
Jeremiah Watson		H L			Br
Dan. Times, Gent.		L			Br
David Valentine		H			Br
George Jeeves		H L	D. Chapman		Br
Timothy Leech	London	H	C. Braybrooke	Ba	
James Smith	Clothall	Hs	Jermyn et al.		Br
Philip Allen		H	John Allen	Ba	
John Day		H		Ba	
Robert Newton		H			Br
William Woosley		H			Br

From Spa Fields to Peterloo

Peace at the end of the wars with France in 1815 did not bring prosperity. Soldiers returning from the wars could not find work; workers who had been employed making such things as guns and army great-coats lost their jobs; manufacturers could not find markets for the goods they were producing; the high price of corn meant that bread was very expensive; and the government was so much in debt that it had to put a tax on such things as candles and tea. Many suffered hardship and distress. There were bread riots and demonstrations against high taxation in many parts of the country. Many radicals (people who wanted to change the whole system at its roots) hoped to channel this discontent into support for parliamentary reform.

Throughout the time when Britain was at war with France, various people had kept the ideas of parliamentary reform alive. One of these people was Major John Cartwright. As early as 1776 he had written a pamphlet which said that Britain would only be the true home of freedom if the parliamentary system was reformed. In particular, he wanted the vote for all adult men and annual elections. Between 1813 and 1815 Major Cartwright began a series of tours in the midlands and north of England. He set up a network of clubs, called Hampden Clubs, for his supporters. This network spread rapidly throughout the country. By March 1817 there were forty Hampden Clubs in the cotton towns of Lancashire alone.

William Cobbett was the son of a Surrey yeoman. In 1802 he began a weekly newspaper called *The Weekly Political Register* which supported the Tories and was generally anti-Reform. But by about 1810 Cobbett had changed his views and was urging reform. In 1816 he found a loophole in the Stamp Duty which put a heavy tax on newspapers. He was able to reduce the price of his *Political Register* from 1s 0½d to 2d, which meant that many more people could afford to buy a copy. His enemies nicknamed the paper the 'Twopenny Trash', but 200,000 of the cheaper copies were sold in the first two months. In the *Political Register* Cobbett urged people to press for a reform of Parliament:

> 'If the skulkers will not join you, if the decent fire-side gentry still keep aloof, proceed by yourselves.'

Henry Hunt, a Wiltshire farmer, became a familiar figure at political meetings. He spoke out strongly in favour of parliamentary reform. 'Orator' Hunt, as he was known, was often asked to speak at large open-air meetings organised by radicals.

Once France had been defeated and the wars were over, the ideas of men like Major John Cartwright, William Cobbett and Henry Hunt became popular again.

The Spa Fields Meetings

A group of extreme reformers, followers of Thomas Spence who wanted to nationalise land and abolish all taxes except income tax, decided to hold a large open-air meeting on Spa Fields, in London. They invited Henry Hunt to speak to the meeting. However, Hunt would only speak if he was allowed to put forward his own view, which was that every adult male should have the vote before anything else at all was reformed. The result was that there were two meetings on Spa Fields – one run by the supporters of Thomas Spence, and the other by Hunt and the radicals. The effect of two great political demonstrations, in one place and at the same time, was too much for some people. Part of the crowd rioted. Shops were broken into, goods were stolen and windows were smashed. A gun shop was raided, and a march on the City of London began. All this was easily stopped by soldiers, but the government used it as an excuse to suspend the Habeas Corpus Act for one year. This is still a very important law. Habeas Corpus (which is Latin for 'have the body produced') means that everybody who is imprisoned has to be brought to trial. The suspension of the Habeas Corpus Act meant that the authorities had the power to put anyone in prison for up to a year without charging them with an offence or even saying that they were there. People could be put in prison for speaking or writing in favour of reform.

The Pentridge Rising

The government made great use of spies and informers to tell them what was happening in various parts of Britain. In the spring of 1817, government spies began sending back reports about a threatened mass revolt in the north of England. The Home Secretary, Lord Sidmouth, sent a spy whose code-name was Oliver, to investigate. 'Oliver' worked with various groups of discontented workers, and tried to convince each group that revolt and revolution was well prepared in every other district but their own. In this way he hoped to bring out into the open those who really wanted to rebel against the government. 'Oliver' was successful. In Huddersfield a few men met together with guns and cudgels, but the group quickly broke up when it became clear that no one anywhere else was supporting them. In Derbyshire, however, it was another matter. Unemployed textile workers, led by Jeremiah Brandreth, set out to link up with other groups (which didn't exist) and capture Nottingham Castle. 'Oliver' had alerted the authorities, and troops were waiting to arrest the marchers. Jeremiah Brandreth and two of his companions were hanged, fourteen were transported, and others were imprisoned.

The Blanketeers

Unemployed workers, mostly weavers, from Manchester planned a great march to London. There they hoped to present a petition to the Prince Regent demanding the reform of Parliament, help for their distress, and the return of Habeas Corpus. The marchers carried blankets in which they slept on their journey, and so were nicknamed 'Blanketeers'. The 'Blanketeers' did not get far. A huge meeting held in St. Peter's Field, Manchester, to cheer them on their way was broken up by troops. The leaders were arrested. Some groups of marchers who had already started were chased, and many men were caught, arrested and thrown into prison without trial. This, of course, could be done because Habeas Corpus had been suspended. Very few marchers got any further than Macclesfield. Only one 'Blanketeer' got through to London.

Peterloo

On 16th August 1819, about 60,000 men, women and children gathered at St. Peter's Field in Manchester. Bands led in groups of men, women and children who carried banners on which were slogans like 'Liberty and Fraternity', 'Reform or Death' and 'Votes for All'. They had all come to listen to Henry Hunt criticise the government and demand parliamentary reform. The local magistrates, who were expecting trouble, had called out the the Manchester Yeomanry. This was a volunteer force, consisting mainly of businessmen and farmers. They stood ready. Standing ready, also, were the regular cavalry in case the yeomanry could not cope. Henry Hunt, sensing that there would be trouble, offered to give himself up. The magistrates preferred to let him speak. When 'Orator' Hunt was well into his speech, the magistrates ordered the yeomanry to arrest him. In the uproar which followed, the cavalry had to force their way through the crowd to rescue the badly trained yeomanry. The results were terrible. Eleven people were killed and hundreds seriously injured, including many women and children.

There was a tremendous outcry in the country. British troops had charged and killed their own people.

The radicals nicknamed the massacre 'Peterloo', in mocking remembrance of the British victory over the French at Waterloo four years earlier. Publicly, the government seemed well pleased. Lord Sidmouth, the Home Secretary, congratulated the magistrates on the action they had taken. Henry Hunt was sent to prison for two years. Privately, however, the government blamed the magistrates for over-reacting. But this did not stop them from using Peterloo as an excuse to attack the radicals.

The Six Acts

There had been nothing illegal about holding the meeting at St. Peter's Field. The government, however, was determined that such a meeting would never be held again. The Six Acts which were passed in 1819 seemed to end all possibilities of peaceful protest. Meetings for the purpose of presenting a petition were limited to the inhabitants of the parish in which the meeting was held; stamp duty was extended to all papers and periodical literature of a certain size, which was a great blow to all kinds of protest literature and particularly to Cobbett's *Political Register*. Magistrates were given wide powers to search private homes for political pamphlets. They were also given the power to try certain cases which previously had to be tried by a judge and jury, and private military training and the collecting of firearms were forbidden.

Altogether, the Six Acts were a very powerful attack upon the radical movement. Legal protest was virtually impossible, and parliamentary reform, in 1820, seemed a long way off.

A contemporary cartoon of the Peterloo massacre, drawn by George Cruikshank. George Cruikshank (1792–1898) came from a family of graphic artists. In his early working life he illustrated children's books and song sheets, and in the 1830s and 1840s drew the pictures for Charles Dickens' stories. Altogether Cruikshank illustrated over 850 books. There was, however, another strand to his work. In 1811 he began drawing satirical cartoons which were usually directed at politicians and political events. Between 1835–54 he published annually George Cruikshank's Comic Almanack which was a comment on the year's political events. The Chartist cartoon on page 30 is from the 1843 edition of the Almanack

Pressure for Reform. People, Political Unions and Press

'Old Sarum', a Reform cartoon published in 1832. The nests represent the rotten boroughs

By 1832 the 'Old Rotten Tree' of Parliament was again under attack. This time the attack was much more powerful. It was organised and was from different groups of people.

The Manufacturing Interest

The manufacturing towns of the midlands and the north were well established by 1815. Gradually, the men who owned and ran the cotton mills and iron foundries, shipyards and nailworks, realised that their own particular interests were not being represented in Parliament. Birmingham manufacturers, for example, realised that their local county MP did not really understand their needs and problems. In 1812 they tried to influence the Warwickshire county election so that the man of their choice was elected. They were unsuc-

cessful, but the idea that they should be represented had taken root. Seven years later, on 10th July 1819, the local paper, the *Edmonds Weekly Recorder and Saturday Advertiser* stated firmly:

> '. . . The people of Birmingham have a right to choose a member or members to sit in the Commons House of Parliament . . .'

Industrialists and manufacturers did not find the existing situation satisfactory. The belief that for them to attempt to influence an election was only a stop-gap measure increased.

Throughout the 1820s the idea grew that a solution would be to redistribute the seats. This would mean that tiny rotten boroughs like Old Sarum and Dunwich (see page 13) would not have a Member of Parliament all to themselves, but that the large industrial towns like Leeds, Manchester, Sheffield and Liverpool would. Some redistribution did happen. In 1821 the seats of Grampound, in Cornwall, were given to Yorkshire – though not to Leeds, as the manufacturers and their supporters had hoped, but to the county. Most reformers thought that this was not enough, and pressed hard for more.

Elections, and Revolution in France

In 1830 a general election was called, and at the same time there was a revolution in France. The Revolution did not influence the election directly, but it helped to keep excitement and interest in politics at fever pitch.

In Yorkshire Henry Brougham was elected to represent the county. This was largely because of the efforts of the manufacturers and merchants, supported by Edward Baines, the editor of the *Leeds Mercury*. They worked hard against the power and influence of the local landowner, Earl Fitzwilliam. Most of Henry Brougham's election campaign speeches were about parliamentary reform. This is part of a speech he made, and which was reported in the *Leeds Mercury* on 27th July 1830:

'Nothing can be more fit than that the manufacturing and commercial interests of this Great Country should have a representative of their own choice to do their business in Parliament. We don't live in the days of Barons, thank God, – we live in the days of Leeds, of Bradford, of Halifax and of Huddersfield – we live in the days when men are industrious and desire to be free; and not when they are lazy and indolent and deserve to be trampled on and dominated over. Therefore you are bound to have your rights and choose your representative.'

Distress in the Towns and in the Countryside

Bad harvests in 1829 and 1830, and a sudden trade slump in 1830 hit rich and poor alike, in towns and in the countryside. The cholera epidemic of 1831–2 made a bad situation worse. Throughout the whole of the 1830–2 period, there were reports from town and country of high poor-rates, high unemployment, poor trade and low wages when employment could be found. In the first three months of 1830 twenty-two county meetings were held to protest about distress or taxation, or both. In February 1830 Earl Grey admitted that the country was in a '. . . state of distress such as never before pressed on any country . . .'.

William Cobbett, the son of a prosperous Surrey farmer, who produced *The Weekly Political Register* and many political pamphlets supporting the poor, toured the country. He wrote in the *Political Register* in early 1832:

'It will be asked, will the reform of Parliament give the labouring man a cow or a pig, will it put bread and cheese into his satchel instead of infernal cold potatoes; will it give him a bottle of beer to carry to the field instead of making him lie down on his belly and drink out of the brook? Will Parliamentary reform put an end to the harnessing of men and women by a hired overseer to draw carts like beasts of burden; will it put an end to the system which causes the honest labourer to be worse fed than the felons in the jails? . . . The enemies of reform jeeringly ask us, whether reform would do all these things for us; and I answer distinctly THAT IT WOULD DO THEM ALL.'

Political Unions

Thomas Attwood, a banker, formed the Birmingham Political Union in 1829. He intended it to be a permanent organisation to focus and lead local reform movements by way of petitions and public meetings. The first meeting of the Birmingham Political Union in January 1830 was attended by 15,000 people; by May 1832 some 100,000 people were attending meetings of the BPU, one quarter of whom were official members.

The Declaration of the Birmingham Political Union stated their position clearly:

'That honourable House [*of Commons*], in its present state, is evidently too far removed in habits, wealth and station [*position*], from the wants and interests of the lower and middle classes of the people, to have . . . any close identity of feeling with them. The great aristocratical interests of all kinds are well represented there . . . But the interests of Industry and of Trade have scarcely any representatives at all!'

Political unions sprang up all over the country. However, while the Birmingham Political Union was able to unite masters and men in one organisation, this did not happen elsewhere. Leeds, for example, had three political unions. Edward Baines, the editor of the *Leeds Mercury*, led the Leeds Association; Joshua Bowers, a glass blower, the Leeds Political Union; while the printers Mann and Frost organised the Leeds Radical Political Union.

Not all the political unions wanted the same kind of reform. In London Francis Place, a tailor from Charing Cross, organised the National Political Union. This union simply wanted the manufacturing interests to be represented in the House of Commons. What was right for the masters, they maintained, was right for the men. On the other hand, William Lovett, a cabinet maker, and Henry Hetherington, the editor of *The Poor Man's Guardian*, wanted nothing less than the vote for every man. They established the National Union of Working Classes.

Clearly the political unions wanted different kinds of parliamentary reform. However, what united the unions was that they all focused public opinion on reform, and in doing so helped to create that public opinion; they showed how this public opinion could be expressed without breaking the law, and they managed to keep public enthusiasm for reform alive and active.

The Press

In March 1830, Earl Grey was blaming the Press for '. . . destroying all respect for rank and station [*position*] and for the institutions of government.' A year later the king, William IV, talked about '. . . the poisonous influence of a licentious and unobstructed press . . .'

Was the Press supporting parliamentary reform? By 1830 many leading London papers were certainly in favour of some kind of reform. *The Times* and the *Examiner* insisted that parliamentary reform was the 'great issue of the moment'; the *Globe* and the *Westminster Review* ran a very full discussion on the British electoral system, whilst the *Morning Chronicle* (usually a very pro-Whig paper) was completely in favour of some kind of reform of both the distribution of seats and of the franchise.

It was, however, in the provinces that newspapers were the most powerful in chanelling local pressure for reform. Parliamentary debates and important speeches by ministers were fully reported. Editors in Manchester, Newcastle and Sheffield commented on what was said in Parliament. Their comments would be read in their own towns, and would both reflect and lead local opinion.

By 1830 some of the larger provincial papers had supported reform for over a generation. Fathers, and now their sons, had written rousing articles and editorials for over twenty years. Men such as Edward Baines and his son (also called Edward) in the *Leeds Mercury*, Thomas and James Thompson in the *Leicester Chronicle* and Charles and Richard Sutton in the *Nottingham Review*, all thundered against a system which did not allow for proper representation from the manufacturing areas. It was the same in the newer provincial papers. John Edward Taylor in the *Manchester Guardian*, Archibald Prentice in the *Manchester Times*, John Foster in the *Leeds Patriot* and Jonathon Crowther in the *Birmingham Journal*, all demanded parliamentary reform of some kind. It was the same on Tyneside with the *Newcastle Chronicle*, on Merseyside with the *Liverpool Mercury* and in Sheffield with the *Sheffield Independent*.

The provincial newspapers were important, not just for their impact upon local opinion, but for their links with the political unions. The Birmingham Political Union, which set the pattern for all others to follow, stated quite clearly that it was the duty of members:

'. . . to consider the means of organising a system of operations whereby the Public Press may be influenced to act generally in support of the public interests. . .'

The link was clear. Members of unions were to work with the local papers in supporting, guiding and leading local opinion.

By 1830 all the indications were clear. The Press, political unions and people were clamouring for a reform of Parliament. Would those inside Parliament listen? Would the members of the House of Commons and the House of Lords pass laws to change the electoral system?

The Struggle in Parliament for Reform

'Depend on it, the country is ripe for revolution . . . then goodbye to England's King and Ministers!'

This warning was contained in an anonymous letter written to the government in 1830. You have read (pages 18–22) about the ways in which pressure for the reform of Parliament was building up in the country. By 1830 the situation was explosive.

The 1830 General Election

King George IV died in the summer of 1830, and, as was the custom, a general election was held. Look back at pages 21–22 to remind yourself of the tensions and excitement which surrounded this election of 1830. Many government supporters were defeated. In constituencies where there were contests, the candidate in favour of a reform of Parliament was elected. Men like Thomas Gooch, who had been MP for Suffolk since 1806, and E.P. Bastard, whose family had held a Devon county seat since 1784, were soundly defeated. In Yorkshire, the Whig Henry Brougham won a spectacular victory. He came from outside Yorkshire (which should have counted against him) and was a strong supporter of parliamentary reform. Yet still he succeeded in gaining one of the county seats.

However, although many MPs who opposed the policies of the Prime Minister were elected, there were not enough of them to bring about a change in government.

Tuesday, 2nd November 1830

The House of Lords was coming to the end of a debate. Earl Grey had made the final speech for the Whig opposition. The Prime Minister, the Tory Duke of Wellington, was well into his speech when he began to defend the electoral system:

'. . . the Legislature [*Parliament*] and the system of representation possess the full and entire confidence of the country . . .'

The Prime Minister seemed to be ignoring the political unions, the great reform rallies and the thundering articles in the Press. Above all, he seemed to be ignoring the results of the summer elections.

Not only was the present system good, Wellington continued, but he had no intention of changing it:

'. . . I am not only not prepared to bring forward any measure of this nature [*reform*], but I will at once declare that . . . I shall always feel it my duty to resist such measures when proposed by others . . .'

The Duke of Wellington had hoped to rally his supporters against the reform of Parliament. That speech had the opposite effect. Tories who had been anxious

The Duke of Wellington, painted by Henry Guttman

before 2nd November were now desperately worried. They joined the Whigs. The fall of the government was certain. A few weeks later, on a minor financial matter, the Tory government of the Duke of Wellington was defeated.

The First Reform Bill

No other Tory leader could form a government which would have the support of the majority of the Members of Parliament. The new king, William IV, therefore asked the Whig leader, Earl Grey, to become Prime Minister.

The Whig government had more aristocrats in it than the previous Tory administration. Yet the Whigs had always seen themselves as reflecting the true interests of the country. Many of them, although aristocrats, were involved in trade and business. The Whigs were very aware of public pressure to introduce far-reaching parliamentary reforms.

On 31st March 1831 the government's proposals were introduced into the House of Commons by Lord John Russell. These proposals were an attempt to shift the balance of representation away from the land-owners and towards the middle classes. Sixty-one boroughs were to lose both their MPs, and forty-seven more were to lose one MP. The number of MPs was to be reduced from 658 to 596, and the remaining forty-six seats were to go to the large manufacturing and in-dustrial towns of the midlands and the north. All the different qualifications which entitled a man to a borough vote were to go. There was to be only one voting qualification: those men living in boroughs and owning or renting a house worth more than £10 a year would be entitled to elect a Member of Parliament.

Outside the House of Commons these proposals were met with enthusiasm. Only Henry Hetherington (editor of *The Poor Man's Guardian*) urged working people to oppose them. He saw that, whilst low wage earners like small shopkeepers and tradesmen would be given the right to elect MPs, most working men still would not have this privilege. Men such as nailmakers, spinners, weavers and farm labourers simply did not live in houses worth £10 a year or more. Other working class leaders, such as Bronterre O'Brien and John Doherty, believed the Reform Bill was the first step towards the kind of electoral reform which they wanted, and urged their followers to support it.

However, it was what happened inside the Houses of Parliament which was important if the Bill was to become law. The debate in the House of Commons was heated. Whigs and Tories spoke against the Bill, and Whigs and Tories spoke in favour. Thomas Babington Macaulay, the Whig MP for the rotten borough of Calne, made a brilliant speech defending the Reform Bill. In it he said:

'. . . we exclude from all share in the government vast masses of property and intelligence, vast numbers of those who are the most interested in preserving tranquillity and who know best how to preserve it. We do more. We drive over to the side of revolution those whom we shut out from power . . . Turn where we may – within, around – the voice of great events is proclaiming to us "Reform, that you may preserve" . . .'

The Tory, Sir Robert Peel, urged caution:

'. . . Let us never be tempted to resign the well tempered freedom which we enjoy, in the ridiculous pursuit of the wild liberty which France has established . . .'

Anti-reformers were terrified by the agitation outside Parliament. They argued that the Bill would destroy the old balance of the constitution.

At the end of the debate, MPs agreed by a majority of just one vote that the Reform Bill should move for-ward to the Committee stage. This meant that a small number of MPs would study it carefully and recommend changes which would amend the Bill before it came back to the Commons again.

Earl Grey was uneasy. A majority of one was not enough. Those opposing the Bill would be able to get amendments passed which would wreck it completely. He was right. The first amendment which was passed objected to the reduction in the total number of MPs. Grey then acted quickly. He persuaded the king, William IV, to dissolve Parliament and call a general election.

The 1831 General Election

The elections proved a great triumph for the reformers. Earl Grey, the Whig Prime Minister, had a majority of 130 seats in the newly elected House of Commons. He did not have to fear any more wrecking amendments in Committee, neither did he have to fear defeat for the Reform Bill in the House of Commons. A second Reform Bill, very like the first, was introduced into the House of Commons in July 1831. It passed through all the stages quickly, and with very little trouble. On 22nd September 1831 the Bill passed its third reading in the House of Commons by 109 votes. It was then sent to the House of Lords.

Battles in the Lords

In order for a Bill to become law, it had to be passed by both the House of Commons and the House of Lords, and then be signed by the king. Earl Grey had been able to get the support of the House of Commons for his Reform Bill, as you have seen. The majority of the members of the House of Lords, however, were against Parliamentary reform.

On 8th October, after a fiery debate lasting five days and nights, the Lords voted on the Reform Bill. They threw it out by a majority of forty-one votes.

The reaction in the country was violent. There were riots in Bristol, Derby, Nottingham and other cities, and in small towns like Blandford in Dorset and Tiverton in Devon. In Leeds a stuffed figure of the Duke of Wellington was burned like Guy Fawkes. The windows of Apsley House, the London home of the Duke of Wellington, were smashed. Radical, reforming newspapers appeared with black borders as a sign of mourning; new political unions were formed in towns which did not already have one, and the older unions increased in size and strength. The Church of England was attacked in the Press: twenty-six bishops sat in the House of Lords, and twenty-one of them had voted against the Reform Bill. Everywhere there were protest marches, and property belonging to anti-reform lords was attacked by stone-throwing mobs.

The Third Reform Bill

In December 1831 Lord John Russell presented the third Reform Bill to the House of Commons. The differences between this Bill and the two previous ones were small. The Bill passed smoothly through all its stages in the House of Commons. For every one MP voting against the Bill, there were two voting in favour.

There remained the House of Lords. Many ministers believed that the only way out of the situation was for the king to create new peers who would be chosen by Grey, and who would support parliamentary reform. There would then be a majority in the House of Lords to out-vote the opponents of reform. Grey and his ministers, however, knew that it would not be easy to persuade William IV to do this. For the time being, though, the Lords seemed as if they were going to be

This picture called 'Bristol Riots Queen Square, October 1831,' was painted by T.L.S Rowbotham and W.J Muller

co-operative. On 13th April 1832 the Lords passed the second reading of the Reform Bill by 184 votes to 175. All seemed to be going well, until an amendment was agreed at the Committee stage which would have meant a delay in discussing which boroughs were to lose MPs.

Grey had had enough. He decided to force the issue and ask William IV to create fifty new peers. William refused, and on 14th April 1832 Earl Grey's Whig government resigned.

The Days of May

Once more the country erupted into riots and rallies. Men like Thomas Attwood and Francis Place (whom you read about on page 21) were determined to stop any likelihood of the Tory leader, the Duke of Wellington, being able to form a government. Westminster was flooded with anti-Tory petitions; the Birmingham Political Union announced that 200,000 men would march on London and stay there until the Bill became law; Francis Place suggested that investors should withdraw all their money from banks at the same time, thus creating an enormous financial crisis. 'Stop the Duke!' 'Go for Gold!' were the slogans written and shouted on the streets of London. It was the same in the provinces.

The *Leeds Mercury* reported gloomily:

'A great Calamity has befallen England
The Boroughmongers have triumphed.
The Reform Bill has been strangled.
The King has refused to make Peers and
The Grey and Brougham administration has
    Resigned.'

The king asked Wellington to investigate the possibility of forming a government which was pledged to limited reforms. However, when Sir Robert Peel, the leading Tory in the House of Commons, refused to serve with him, Wellington knew that he would not succeed in his task. Four days later he told the king that he was unable to form a government. William IV, who had never formally accepted Grey's resignation, asked Grey to take over again. He promised Grey he would create as many peers as would be needed to get the Reform Bill through the House of Lords.

The Bill becomes Law

In the event it was not necessary to create any new peers. The threat was enough. Once new peers were created, they would be there for always. There would, therefore, always be a Whig majority in the Lords. Whig bills which had passed the Commons would not be able to be stopped in the Lords, and would almost automatically become law. The Tory Lords could not tolerate this possibility. On 4th July 1832, when the Reform Bill came up for its final reading in the House of Lords, most of the lords who had opposed Earl Grey and the Whig administration stayed away. The Reform Bill was passed by 106 votes to 22.

King William IV signed the Bill on 7th June 1832. The Reform Bill became the Reform Act of 1832.

The Reform Act of 1832

Earl Grey and the Whig supporters had been successful in bringing about parliamentary reform. Throughout the long struggle, however, it was clear that Grey wanted reform because he believed that moderate reform was the only way to real political stability. Grey and the Whigs wanted to keep a system where government was in the hands of men of property. They believed that all men owning or renting property worth a reasonable amount of money should have the privilege of voting for their representatives in Parliament. The Whigs and their supporters believed that property owners would want the country to be stable in order to protect what they owned; those with money to rent a reasonably sized house for themselves and their family, would hardly want to join a revolution which might end up with them losing what little they had.

The Reform Act of 1832 brought important changes in two main areas: the franchise and the distribution of seats.

The Franchise: Who Could Vote?

The right to vote, whether a man lived in a county or in a borough, was still based on property.

In the counties, two new groups of people were added to those who could vote already. These two new groups were men who were copyholders (an old kind of lease) of land worth £10 a year, and men who were leaseholders of land worth £50 a year. After 1832 about one adult man in five was entitled to vote, compared with one in ten beforehand. Most of the new voters were small property owners.

In the boroughs, all the old systems of deciding who could vote and who could not were thrown out and replaced by a single qualification. All adult men occupying property worth at least £10 a year were entitled to vote. Of course, the value of property was different in different parts of the country. In London, where rents were high, many skilled workers could vote. In Birmingham, only 7,000 workers out of a population of 144,000 lived in houses worth more than £10 a year; in Manchester, the figure was 13,000 from a population of 182,000 and in Leeds, 5,000 from a population of 125,000.

The Distribution of Seats

There was a shift in the distribution of seats from the south to the industrial north. Fifty-six rotten boroughs in the south and west of England no longer sent MPs to Westminster, and thirty boroughs lost one of their MPs. By and large these seats were given to the north. Towns such as Sheffield, Leeds and Manchester sent an MP to Parliament for the first time. But some pocket boroughs survived: between sixty and seventy MPs were in the House of Commons after 1832 because some other person of influence wanted them there.

SOURCE WORK:
Parliamentary Reform

SOURCE A

The "System" that "Works so Well"! – or The Boroughmongers GRINDING Machine.

1. In this cartoon by Cruikshank (Source A) the building called 'St. Stephens' represents Parliament.
   (a) Who are the people who benefit from 'the system'?
   (b) What is 'the system' which they say is 'working so well'?
   (c) Which other groups of people, apart from those illustrated in the cartoon, also benefitted from 'the system'?
   You will need to look back at pages 12–15 to help you answer this question.

SOURCE B

'The measure proposed is an effective one. It cuts off obvious and disgusting abuses . . .

No one can deny but that whatever is in the bill is good.

To the House we should say, 'Pass it, pass it.'

To the people, 'Urge in every way the passing of the bill; call for it, press it forward.'

Let the public cast their eyes over the list of rotten boroughs, as contained in Lord John Russell's speech. Their mock representatives will not much longer insult the commonsense of all mankind, by retaining seats in a British House of Commons to pass laws which are to bind the men of England.'

(From the leading article in *The Times*, 2nd March 1831)

SOURCE C

'I have been uniformly opposed to reform on principle, because I was unwilling to open a door which I saw no prospect of being able to close. . .

I will continue my opposition to the last, believing, as I do, that this is the first step, not directly to revolution, but to a series of changes which will affect the property, and totally change the character . . . of this country . . . we may establish a republic full of energy – splendid in talent – but in my conscience I believe fatal to our liberty, our security and our peace.'

(From *The Speeches of Sir Robert Peel*, vol ii, 1853. Debate on the second reading of the Second Reform Bill, 17th December 1831)

2. Read Sources B and C carefully.
   (a) What *advantages* did *The Times* believe reform would bring?
   (b) What *disadvantages* did Sir Robert Peel believe reform would bring?

3. How important were newspapers in the campaign for parliamentary reform? (It will help you to look back at page 22 when you are thinking about your answer.)

Parliamentary Reform

SOURCE D

In 1831 Lord John Russell wrote to Edward Baines, who was the editor of the *Leeds Mercury*. He asked Edward Baines to find out what would happen if the vote was given to men owning, or living in, property worth more than £10 a year. Baines got the information from thirty canvassers who had worked for the Whigs in the 1831 election. This source is part of his reply, written on 7th November 1831.

'. . . they were surprised to find how few comparatively would be allowed to vote. . . It appeared that in the parts occupied chiefly by the working classes, not one householder in 50 would have a vote. In the streets occupied by shops, almost every householder had a vote. . . In the township of Holbeck, containing 11,000 inhabitants, chiefly of the working classes, but containing several mills, dye-houses, public houses, and respectable dwellings, there are only 150 voters. . . Out of 140 householders, heads of families, working in the mill of Messrs Marshall and Co., there are only two who will have the vote. . . Out of 160 or 170 householders in the mill of Messrs O. Willans and Sons, Holbeck, there is not one vote; out of the about 100 householders in the employment of Messrs Taylor and Wordsworth, machine makers, – the highest class of mechanic, – only one has the vote. It appeared that of the working classes, not more than one in fifty would be enfranchised by the Bill. . .

. . . there will be in the borough of Leeds, the population of which is 124,000, the number of 6,683 voters. Making the deduction for female householders and uninhabited houses . . . I should think the number of voters will be reduced to less than 5,000 . . . I need not remark to your Lordship, that if the proportion of voters is comparatively so small in such a town as Leeds, it must be still smaller in less populous places.'

(From E. Baines, jnr., *Life of Edward Baines*, 2nd edn., 1859)

4. Read Source D carefully, and look back at the section called 'The Struggle in Parliament for Reform' on pages 22–5.
   (a) Why would Lord John Russell have written to Edward Baines *at this time*?
   (b) How likely was it that Edward Baines would have given accurate information in answer to Lord John Russell's question?
   (c) Did the information supplied to Lord John Russell support the Whig view of parliamentary reform?

SOURCE E

The following extracts are from the diary (1831) of John Campbell, a Whig MP for Stafford.

2nd March We are quite appalled. There is not the remotest chance of such a bill being passed by this or any House of Commons . . . This really is a revolution. . .
   The general sentiment is that the measure [*Bill*] goes a good deal too far. It is applauded [*praised*] by the radicals and *some* Whigs, but it is very distasteful to a great part of the Whig party.
3rd March The general belief is that the Bill must be thrown out on the second reading. I expect Ministers will then resign and anarchy [*break-down of law and order*] begin . . . I feel inclined as a choice of evils to support and even speak in favour of the Bill.
5th March The measure takes very much with the country.
8th March I still consider the Bill dangerously violent, but apprehend [*feel there is*] less danger from passing it than from rejecting it.
27th March The *chance* of the Bill being carried by the present Parliament is the *certainty* that it would be carried by the new Parliament.'

(J. Hardcastle, ed., *Life of John, Lord Campbell, vol.i, 1881.*)

5. John Campbell clearly changed his mind! Use your knowledge of what was happening in the country at the time to explain the reasons he might have had for doing this.

6. An historian is investigating the reasons behind the events in Parliament of 1831–2 which ended in the passing of the Reform Act of 1832.
   Explain which of the following sources this historian would find the most useful:
   (i) *Hansard*, the official record of the House of Commons;
   (ii) the diary of the Whig MP, John Campbell;
   (iii) copies of the newspaper, the *Leeds Mercury*, dated between 1830 and 1832.

7. Why was the Reform Act passed in 1832?

The Chartists: Beginnings to 1840

The Six Points
OF THE
PEOPLE'S
CHARTER.

1. A VOTE for every man twenty-one years of age, of sound mind, and not undergoing punishment for crime.

2. THE BALLOT.—To protect the elector in the exercise of his vote.

3. No PROPERTY QUALIFICATION for Members of Parliament —thus enabling the constituencies to return the man of their choice, be he rich or poor.

4. PAYMENT OF MEMBERS, thus enabling an honest trades-man, working man, or other person, to serve a constituency, when taken from his business to attend to the interests of the country.

5. EQUAL CONSTITUENCIES, securing the same amount of representation for the same number of electors, instead of allowing small constituencies to swamp the votes of large ones.

6. ANNUAL PARLIAMENTS, thus presenting the most effectual check to bribery and intimidation, since though a constituency might be bought once in seven years (even with the ballot), no purse could buy a constituency (under a system of universal suffrage) in each ensuing twelvemonth; and since members, when elected for a year only, would not be able to defy and betray their constituents as now.

A chartist hand-bill

In the ten years between 1838 and 1848 handbills like this one were to be seen on the streets of Birmingham, Manchester, London, Leeds and other large towns. Where did they come from? Who wanted yet more change so soon after the Reform Act of 1832, and why?

The Reform Act of 1832 had increased the numbers of voters. Before 1832 one in ten adult men in England and Wales could vote; after 1832 the number had increased to one in five. Most of the new voters, how-ever, were owners of small properties. What Grey and the Whigs wanted to preserve above all things was that government should continue to be in the hands of men of property, and this they had done. In the first general election after the 1832 Reform Act had been passed, between 70 per cent and 80 per cent of those elected represented the landed interest. Only about 100 MPs were bankers, merchants or manufacturers.

The Working Men's Association and the Charter

Many were angered by what they saw as a series of betrayals by the government which at one time had seemed to promise them so much.

Francis Place, (see page 21) joined with a cabinet maker called William Lovett and six radical MPs to form the London Working Men's Association. This Associ-ation first met in June 1836. William Lovett, who was then aged thirty-six, was its secretary, and Henry Hetherington (see page 23) was treasurer. From the start the Association aimed to bring about change by persuasion, and not through riots and violent demon-strations. Their programme was set out in the People's Charter, which was written by William Lovett. The London Working Men's Association (LWMA) held public meetings, formed discussion groups and produced pamphlets. They hoped that by using moral, not physical, force, Parliament would accept the Six Points of the Charter. 'Before an educated people', Wil-liam Lovett declared, 'a government must bow.'

Disappointment, anger and frustration with the reforms of the Whig government were being expressed, too, in other parts of the country. In the north of England Feargus O'Connor, an Irish landowner and ex-MP, thundered against what he saw as the evils of the government. His speeches roused huge crowds to fury. He insisted that the only way to have fairer laws was to give working class people the vote. His newspaper, the *Northern Star*, which was published in Leeds, car-ried the same message and was read throughout the north.

People who became Chartists were craftsmen such as printers, tailors and cabinet makers, factory workers such as the cotton-spinners of Bolton and the wool-combers of Bradford, and domestic outworkers such as handloom weavers, framework knitters and nail-makers.

London was an important Chartist centre, and so was Birmingham, with the support of Thomas Attwood and the Birmingham Political Union. Men and women in towns and villages throughout England, Wales and Scotland supported Chartism at different times and for different reasons. Some men and women turned to Chartism when times were bad. When trade was poor and wages fell and unemployment was high, they looked to Chartism to solve their problems. Some difficulties were entirely local. Manchester cotton operatives were thrown out of work for several months at a time if the American cotton crop failed. Many turned to Chartism as a result. Yet this particular problem would not affect, for example, the framework knitters of Leicester. They had their own problems which led many of them into the Chartist movement, if only for a short period of time. There were, of course, hundreds of men and women who were Chartists in good times as well as in bad. Whatever the reasons for people becoming Char-tists, they all believed that to get working men into the House of Commons as MPs would be the only long-term solution to their problems. Somehow Parliament had to be persuaded to accept the Six Points of the People's Charter.

In 1838 all the various Chartist groups gathered together at a great rally held at Holloway Head in Bir-mingham on 6th August. The rally accepted the Six Points of the People's Charter. It was agreed that Char-tists would collect signatures for a national petition in support of the Charter, and that if Parliament rejected the Petition there would be a general strike – a 'sacred month'. They agreed, too, that there would be a national Chartist Convention. Members would be chosen by the Chartist groups around the country, and would meet to prepare for the presentation of the Petition to Parliament.

The Convention

The Chartist Convention met in London in February 1839, and quickly settled down to business. Almost immediately there were difficulties. Members discussed whether they could deal only with the Petition, or whether they could act as if they were a 'People's Parliament', and discuss other matters which were important to them. Perhaps most significant of all, they talked about the tactics they would adopt if Parliament rejected the Petition and the Charter. Here they were hopelessly divided. Some Chartists favoured using physical force if necessary; others believed strongly that moral force, persuasion, was the only way. O'Connor declared:

'We have resolved to obtain our rights, peacefully if we may, forcibly if we must.'

Some Chartists were arming themselves and preparing to fight the authorities. Ben Wilson, in a book he wrote which was published in 1887 called *The Struggles of an old Chartist*, said:

'A great many people in these districts were arming themselves with guns or pikes, and drilling on the moors. Bill Cockroft, one of the leaders of the physical force party in Halifax, wished me to join the movement, I consented, and purchased a gun, although I knew it to be a serious thing for a Chartist to have a gun or pike in his possession.'

William Lovett was to remember, in his autobiography written in 1876:

'The whole physical force agitation is harmful and injurious to the movement. Muskets are not what is wanted, but education and schooling of the working people. . . O'Connor wants to take everything by storm, and to pass Charter into Law within a year. All this hurry and haste, this bluster and menace of armed opposition can only lead to the destruction of Chartism.'

Were the Chartists to carry weapons and try by force to persuade Parliament to do what they wanted? Disgusted with the way the discussion seemed to be going, William Lovett and the 'moral force' Chartists walked out. The Convention promptly moved to Birmingham and waited.

The government was by now thoroughly alarmed at the talk in the Convention, and at rumours that armed Chartist groups were drilling with sticks, cudgels and guns. In 1839 they put Major General Sir Charles Napier in charge of 5,000 soldiers and gave him the responsibility of keeping law and order in the north.

The government was determined that no revolution of the French kind would happen in Britain.

The First Petition

The first Chartist national petition was enormous. It was three miles long and contained 1,280,000 signatures. It was presented to the House of Commons in July 1839 by John Fielden and Thomas Attwood, who were both MPs. The Commons, however, by a vote of 235 to 46 refused even to consider it. The Chartist Convention ordered the 'sacred month' to begin, but by now even Feargus O'Connor was against it:

'. . . the baker will not bake, the butcher will not kill, and the brewer will not brew; then what becomes of the millions of starving human beings?'

The 'sacred month' was cancelled by the Convention, which dissolved itself at the end of August. The possibility of organised protest and pressure for change seemed to have been lost.

The Newport Rising

Once Parliament had rejected the Petition, various local Chartist groups took matters into their own hands. Suspicion and rumour were everywhere. Some of the rumours were begun by government agents, others by the Chartists themselves. In some towns, buildings and troops were stoned; in others, hand-to-hand fighting broke out between Chartists and police or troops. Some incidents, however, were more serious.

It was rumoured that there was a plan to capture key towns in South Wales and establish a republic there. On the night of 3–4 November 1839, John Frost, who had been the Newport delegate at the Convention, and others led 7,000 miners and ironworkers in a march on Newport. Their immediate aim was to free a fellow worker from gaol. However, the whole affair was totally mismanaged. The Chartists did not reach the town until daybreak, and when they did, they found a strong force of government troops waiting for them in the Westgate Hotel.

After a short, fierce battle the Chartists were dispersed. Twenty-four people were killed or died of their injuries and 125 were arrested. Among those arrested was John Frost, who was charged with treason and condemned to death.

By 1840, then, the Chartist movement seemed to have collapsed. Parliament had refused to consider the Charter. Troops and police had mopped up the rioting which had occurred, and many ordinary Chartists had seen the inside of a prison for the first time. Chartist leaders, including William Lovett and Feargus O'Connor, were in prison. Others, like John Frost, had had their death sentences changed to transportation for life. There seemed to be no way in which working people could force the government to listen to them.

The Chartists: 1840-48

The Second Petition

Despite the government's attempts to silence the Chartists, the movement was far from dead. Feargus O'Connor began to re-organise. He founded the National Charter Association in 1840, which had 48,000 members within two years. They decided to collect signatures for yet another petition to support the Charter. The pressure was on the government again. Unemployment rose in 1842, particularly in the north, and the Chartists easily collected over three million signatures from working people determined to make Parliament pay attention to them.

The Petition, carried by fifty men, was delivered to the House of Commons in May 1842. The House of Commons debated whether or not they would accept the Chartists' Petition, and decided not to by 287 votes to 49. The Petition, and with it the Charter, was again rejected.

This page from George Cruikshank's Comic Almanack for 1843 shows that not everyone took the Chartists seriously. How does George Cruikshank manage to poke fun at the Chartists? Do you think he is giving a true account of a real party?

1843.]   FEBRUARY.   9

A CHARTER PARTY.

THE United Female Chartist Washerwomen met a deputation from the Infant Society of Universal Suffrage and Vote by Ballot Orphans, in the long room of the Institution belonging to the former, when a discussion ensued on the subject of the Charter.

It was at length resolved to extend the five *pints* to six ; and it was finally agreed, that three quarts should constitute the measure they are jointly going for.

Upon a proposition that they should adopt the principle of the whole hog, a discussion arose as to whether the gammon was to be included ; but it was soon decided that the whole hoggites would be nothing at all, if it were not for the gammon, which was accordingly retained by a large majority.

The following subscriptions, in aid of the " Victim Fund," were then read by the secretary, who stated, that the amounts were in the hands of the treasurer, who was absent from indisposition :

Subscriptions to the " Victim Fund."

	£	s.	d.
Eight-and-twenty patriotic mothers	0	0	9
Three charwomen, who are ready to scour the country in aid of the good cause	0	0	3
Nine tailors, who feel as one man	0	0	1
Ten patriotic grandmothers, who would see their grandchildren enjoying their freedom in the land of their grandfathers	0	0	5
The hands employed upon St. Martin's clock	0	0	6

The great petition was then brought forward for additional signatures, when it was resolved, that knowing how to write should not be a *sine quâ non* for signing it. Several chartist children were permitted to put their marks, and the grand master of the lodge of juvenile levellers was appointed as controller of the sand and blotting paper.

In the evening tea was served, and several rounds of patriotic toasts were given.

Plug Plots

The Chartists were disappointed and angry that yet again Parliament refused even to listen. They became even more angry when an industrial depression again hit the midlands and the north. Mills and factories could not sell their goods. At Ashton-under-Lyne and Stalybridge, near Manchester, the owners of the cotton mills reduced the wages they paid to their workers because they were not able to sell the goods which were produced. Other factory owners, in similar situations, did the same. A wave of strikes began, which quickly spread across the Pennines to Yorkshire. Striking workers managed to cause chaos by pulling the plugs from the steam boilers which worked machinery in factories and pumped water out of mines. If the steam boilers would not work, neither could the mines and factories.

Many, but not all, of the strikers and their leaders were Chartists. Some were simply protesting about the way in which they were being treated by the mill and factory owners. Some Chartists, however, regarded the strikes as an ideal opportunity to show working people that the Charter was the only way of getting their voice heard in Parliament.

Still the government did not listen. There were local skirmishes between strikers and troops or police; strikers were imprisoned or transported. Hunger forced many back to work, and the 'Plug Plots' collapsed. It seemed that all the government had to do was wait. They could not be forced to listen to the Chartists nor to the starving strikers.

Education, Religion and Land

Chartist leaders were not able to make the government listen, but they were able to carry on trying to improve the lives of ordinary working people.

While they were in Warwick gaol, William Lovett and a fellow Chartist called John Collins worked on their idea that working people could only improve their situation through education. They wanted to see 'The National Association of the United Kingdom for Promoting the Political and Social Improvement of the People' organise branches throughout the country. In the event, only one, in London, was set up in 1842. A year later William Lovett established a Sunday School, which gradually became the centre for his educational ideas.

Some Chartists became missionaries who travelled the length and breadth of the country, preaching and teaching that '. . .Every Christian must be a Chartist, and that all will be better Chartists for being Christians.' Huge meetings were held in Wales and the West Country, in Yorkshire, the midlands, and in Scotland. Sometimes these meetings were held in the open air; sometimes they were held in church halls which had been loaned by sympathetic clergymen; and sometimes they were held in special, separate Chartist churches.

Feargus O'Connor would have none of this. His way of helping the poor was to help them own their own land. His idea was that Chartists should buy shares in the National Land Company, which he set up in 1845. The money would be used to buy land. The shareholders would draw lots to see which of them could settle on the land. The idea was very popular; at least 70,000 Chartists bought shares and about 250 of these actually settled on land which had been bought by the Company. However, O'Connor knew very little about running a company of this kind, and soon the whole enterprise collapsed in financial disaster.

Women Chartists

In many areas, for example the weaving villages of Lancashire and Yorkshire, Chartism became a family affair. Fathers and sons would attend political meetings together, and sisters, wives and mothers would provide back-up support. This involved, for example, making tea at meetings, packing lunches and dinners, and sewing banners.

However, women also began to become involved in the political side of Chartism. Between 1837 and 1844 over eighty Political Unions and Chartist Associations were formed which were for women only. These Unions and Associations did not try to encourage women to be speakers at rallies nor to be political agitators. Rather, they tried to find new ways in which the women could support the political ambitions of their sons and fathers. Chartist leaders believed that the surest way to gain the Six Points of the People's Charter was to 'enlist the sympathies and quicken the intellects of our wives and children.'

Yet Chartists like Ernest Jones and R. G. Gammage, when they were later writing down their memories of Chartism, were sad that they had not paid more attention to the women and children in the movement. They believed, too late, that it was the women and children who held the key to working-class progress. Perhaps, however, they would not go quite as far as their contemporary, Caroline Maria Williams, who declared 'The Charter will never become the law of the land until we women are fully resolved that it shall be so.'

The Third Petition

However, the Charter had not been forgotten by the Chartist leaders nor by the Chartists themselves. They had failed twice to get Parliament to listen to them. In 1848, however, the government was in a mood to take the Chartists seriously.

1847 had been a hard year. Many businesses had collapsed, and there was a great deal of unemployment and poverty. Thousands of people were forced to depend on the new Poor Law, which they hated. Steadily support for the Charter grew again until, in the spring of 1848, Feargus O'Connor declared that there were 6 million signatures on a new petition. An enormous mass meeting on Kennington Common in London was planned, after which the Chartists were to march to Parliament demanding that the Charter should become law.

1848 was a fateful year for the governments of Europe. The King of France was overthrown, and this event was quickly followed by revolutions in most European countries. In Britain the government took the Chartists seriously. But it was not the Charter which they took seriously. They took seriously what they saw as the Chartist threat to law and order. The government was afraid that a European-style revolution, spearheaded by the Chartists, would begin in Britain.

The Duke of Wellington was put in charge of the defence of London: 8,000 soldiers were called up, along with 1,500 Chelsea Pensioners (who were all ex-soldiers), and 150,000 special constables were enrolled. Clearly the government was expecting trouble on a vast scale from the Kennington Common meeting, and was taking no chances. The police, fearing the worst, asked Feargus O'Connor to deliver the Petition to Parliament by himself and not at the head of a large, and possibly threatening, procession of Chartists. O'Connor, perhaps afraid that he could not himself control vast hordes of Chartists if they became violent, agreed.

The government had over-estimated. Only about 20,000 Chartists marched to Kennington Common, not the 500,000 for which Feargus O'Connor had hoped. There they listened peacefully to the speakers, and went home quietly afterwards. The great Chartist Petition was delivered to Parliament by Feargus O'Connor alone, and was carried there in three cabs. There was no violence, and certainly no move to overthrow the government by force.

This time government officials did read the Petition. The signatures were counted and inspected. The officials found that, far from 6 million, there were slightly less than 2 million actual signatures. Some names were clearly made up; others were poor forgeries. 'Queen Victoria', 'Flat Nose', 'Pug Face' and 'Mr Punch' could not have signed the Petition! Some names were so rude that they were not even put in *Hansard*, the official record of Parliament. In this way the Petition became a joke, and the government was able to avoid considering the serious demands made by the Charter itself.

There were no more mass meetings, no more petitions. Chartism was over. Some of the older Chartists, like R. G. Gammage, retired from the fray to write down their memoirs. Other Chartists joined newly developing organisations such as trade unions and co-operative societies. These were, in different ways, also pressing for improvement in the lives of ordinary working men and women.

The Importance of the Chartist Movement

The Chartists had failed to gain the Six Points of the People's Charter. They had failed, even, to persuade Parliament to debate them. They had, however, achieved a great deal. For the first time in Britain,

The Chartist meeting on Kennington Common, 1848

working people had organised themselves, not just to hold meetings and sign petitions as part of a political campaign to gain the Charter, but also to run churches, schools and a land scheme; to organise outings, tea parties and soup kitchens; and to produce handbills, pamphlets and a newspaper. They had given themselves hope, and they had shown to others something of their strength and determination.

The Chartist settlement of Snig's End near Gloucester, drawn for the Illustrated London News *in 1850*

SOURCE WORK:
The Chartists

1. Read the handbill 'The Six Points of the People's Charter' on page 28.
   Explain carefully which Point, or Points, would make sure that:
   (i) a man who depended on a regular job for his income could give up that job in order to become an MP;
   (ii) a man who was not rich enough to own a house or land could become an MP;
   (iii) men would be free to vote for whoever they wanted, without being afraid that their employer or landlord would find out;
   (iv) there was no more bribery at elections.

2. Was disappointment with the Reform Act the *only* reason the Chartist movement began?

Chartism in the North of England

SOURCE A

General Sir Charles Napier was appointed to command the troops in the Northern District (northern England) in April 1839. These extracts are taken from his diary, and were written between 6th August 1839 and 12th January 1840.

'6.8.1839
Poor people! They will suffer. They have set all England against them and their physical force: fools! We have the physical force, not they. They talk of their hundred thousands of men. Who is to move them when I am dancing round them with cavalry, and pelting them with cannonshot? What would their 100,000 men do with my 100 rockets wriggling their fiery tails among them, roaring, scorching, tearing, smashing all they came near?

1.12.1839
An anonymous letter came, with a Chartist plan. Poor creatures, their threats of attack are miserable. With half a cartridge, and half a pike, with no money, no discipline, no skilful leaders, they would attack men with leaders, money and discipline, well armed, and having sixty rounds a man. Poor men! A republic! What good did a republic ever do? What good will it ever do?

2.12.1839
The streets of this town are horrible. The poor starving people go about by twenties and forties, begging, but without the least insolence; and yet some rich villains, and some foolish women, choose to say they try to exhort charity. It is a lie, an infernal lie, neither more nor less: – nothing can exceed the good behaviour of these poor people, except it be their cruel sufferings.

3.12.1839
Spoke to the mayor about a subscription: – the excellent mayor, Mr. Roworth. He joins me in all my opinions as to the thrice-accursed new poor law, its bastilles and its guardians. Lying title! They guard nothing, not even their own carcasses, for they so outrage misery that if a civil war comes they will be immediately sacrificed.

12.1.1840
Patrolled all last night. Saw the Chartist sentinels in the streets; we knew they were armed with pistols, but I advised the magistrates not to meddle with them. Seizing these men could do no good; it would not stop Chartism if they were all hanged, and they offered no violence; why starve their wretched families and worry them with a long imprisonment?'

(From General Napier's diaries, quoted in Charles Napier, *Life of General Sir Charles Napier*, 1857)

3. Read Source A carefully.
   (a) What evidence is there in this source that General Napier was:
      (i) sympathetic;
      (ii) unsympathetic towards the Chartists?

   (b) How reliable is General Sir Charles Napier's diary as a source of evidence about:
      (i) his attitude towards the Chartists?
      (ii) Chartist activity in the north of England?

The Chartists

Chartism in Wales

SOURCE B

'A company of the 45th Regiment was stationed at the Westgate Hotel, and thither the multitude marched, loudly cheering as they proceeded through the streets. Arrived in front of the Hotel, an attack was immediately commenced; the magistrates, police, and specials were driven from the streets, and fled into the Hotel for refuge. The soldiers were stationed at the windows, through which a number of people began to fire . . . The soldiers, as a matter of course, returned the fire . . . the consequence was, that in about twenty minutes ten of the Chartists were killed on the spot, and about fifty others wounded.'

(From R.G. Gammage, *History of the Chartist Movement*, 1854)

SOURCE C

4. Look carefully at Source C which is a painting of the Newport riots.
   (a) Make a list of the ways in which Sources B and C agree.
   (b) Make a list of the ways in which Sources B and C disagree.
   (c) How would you explain the differences between the sources?

SOURCE D

This extract is taken from the official record of the trial of John Frost. It is part of the evidence given by Edward Patton, a carpenter from Newport.

'The parcel of people I saw in the morning of the riot, were armed; they had guns, sticks, etc.; the sticks had iron points, I did not see many with guns. I saw of this body two hundred or three hundred. There were not many more. I had full view of those on Stowe Hill . . . I know the two bow-windows in front of the Westgate. I never saw anything done to the windows of the Westgate. I did not hear a crash of windows. They were not very tumultuous. They drew up in front of the Westgate. I am certain they said the prisoners were taken before daylight. It was about nine o'clock in the morning when they came down Stowe Hill. It was broad daylight two hours before that. Those that were in the Westgate were taken before daylight. The body of the mob stood for a space, and asked for the prisoners who were taken before daylight. None of the mob went forward as spokesman. They came close to the door. I could only see the steps, to which the mob came close up. The first moment or two they asked for the prisoner Smith; then a rush was made. Then I heard firing, and took to my heels. I cannot say whether the mob had guns, or pikes or clubs. I cannot tell whether they were armed for the biggest part. I hears some one say, in a very loud voice, 'No, never.' I was distant from the door of the Westgate twenty-five yards when I heard the words. I heard no groaning. I could not say where the firing began. No man could judge. You nor I could not tell. Saw no smoke outside. It is likely enough that the firing began from the Westgate Inn.'

(From the *Northern Star*, 5th July 1839)

5. Now read Source D. Does Edward Patton's evidence make you believe that the painting or Source B is the more likely to be an accurate account of what happened in Newport in November 1839? Use the sources and your own knowledge to help you explain your answer.

The Chartists

Women Chartists

SOURCE E

'FELLOW-COUNTRY WOMEN,
We have been told that the province of woman is her home, and that the field of politics should be left to men; this we deny; . . . Is it not true that the interests of our fathers, husbands, and brothers ought to be ours? If they are oppressed and impoverished, do we not share those evils with them? If so, ought we not to resent the infliction of those wrongs upon them?

For years we have struggled to maintain our homes in comfort, such as our hearts told us should greet our husbands after their fatiguing labours. Year after year have passed away, and even now our wishes have no prospect of being realised, our husbands are over wrought, our houses half furnished, our families ill-fed, and our children uneducated – the fear of want hangs over our heads; the scorn of the rich is pointed towards us; . . . We are a despised caste; our oppressors are not content with despising our feelings, but demand the control of our thoughts and wants! . . . – we are oppressed because we are poor . . .'

('Address of the Female Political Union Newcastle-upon-Tyne to their Fellow-countrywomen, published in the *Northern Star*, 9th February 1839)

6. What does this source tell you about:
   (i) the ways in which these women from Newcastle viewed their lives?
   (ii) the attitude of these women to the Chartist movement?

7. What was the attitude of the Chartist movement towards women? Use this source and your own knowledge to explain your answer.

What Might Happen

SOURCE F

THE CHARTER – A Common's Scene.

8. This cartoon shows what the political cartoonist George Cruikshank thought Parliament would be like if the Six Points of the People's Charter ever became law. Use the sources in this chapter and your own knowledge to explain whether or not you agree with him.

2
UTILITARIANISM

The Greatest Happiness of the Greatest Number of People

'Utilitarianism' is the nineteenth-century name given to an idea developed by Jeremy Bentham (1748–1832). It attracted many, but by no means all, of those involved in making new laws or putting forward new schemes for such things as education, prisons and the Poor Law. It is helpful to study him because leading politicians and men who worked in administrative posts in the first half or two-thirds of the nineteenth century were often affected by Jeremy Bentham and his ideas about Utilitarianism.

Jeremy Bentham (1748–1832)

Jeremy Bentham was born in London in 1748. His father, Jeremiah, was a prosperous solicitor, and Jeremy was sent to Westminster School and then to Queen's College, Oxford. He was going to become a lawyer. However, by the time he was twenty, Jeremy Bentham had decided upon his life's work. Quite by chance, while in a coffee-house in Oxford, he picked up a pamphlet called *Essay on Government* by Joseph Priestley. In this pamphlet he found the phrase 'The greatest happiness of the greatest number'. Bentham later wrote:

'It was by that pamphlet and this phrase in it that my principles on the subject of morality, public and private, were determined.'

From that moment onwards, Bentham decided that he would devote the whole of his life to building a scientific and logical foundation for the laws which should govern the lives of people in society. He had, first, to produce a sound foundation for any possible legal system. Secondly, he had to use this theoretical foundation to criticise existing legal systems and laws.

In 1789 Bentham published his *Introduction to the Principles of Morals and Legislation*. This begins with a very clear statement which was basic to Bentham's thinking about the law:

'Nature has placed mankind under the governance of two sovereign masters, pain and pleasure. It is for them alone to point out what we ought to do, as well as determine what we shall do . . . They govern us in all we do, in all we say, in all we think. . .'

In other words, Jeremy Bentham decided that all human feelings could be divided into two: those which gave pleasure and those which gave pain.

Bentham went on to say that all actions and all laws can be judged by using his 'Principle of Utility'. This principle would show whether the law had utility (or usefulness) in bringing about the happiness of the greatest possible number of people.

'By utility is meant that property in any object, whereby it tends to produce benefit, advantage, pleasure, good, or happiness . . . or to prevent the happening of mischief, pain, evil, or unhappiness to the party whose interest is considered: if that party be the community in general, then the happiness of the community: if a particular individual, then the happiness of that individual . . .'

So Utilitarianism was a form of test to decide which laws were good and which were bad. Furthermore, the test of what laws there ought to be, and which laws ought to be obeyed, was also a matter of utility – did they increase the sum of human happiness?

At the same time that he was writing his *Introduction to the Principles of Morals and Legislation*, Bentham began putting some of his ideas into practice. He started work on plans for a prison, the Panopticon, based on a completely new design. There were serious proposals to build this prison, but the whole enterprise eventually came to nothing. Even so, it was an important venture because it showed that Bentham believed his ideas could be put to practical use. It was also important because it turned Bentham into a believer in democracy. Bentham argued that only a parliament which did not really represent the people and which, therefore, did not have the people's best interests at heart could possibly turn down such an advantageous scheme as his Panopticon!

Gradually, Jeremy Bentham became involved with a group of writers who thought as he did. These 'Utilitarians' wrote and addressed meetings on political and social matters. Bentham himself wrote many pamphlets urging reform and exposing abuses. He thus had a considerable influence upon the sort of laws which were being agreed by Parliament in the early years of the nineteenth century. All this time Bentham was also steadily at work on his *Constitutional Code*, which he hoped would be of use to all those involved in making laws.

Jeremy Bentham died in 1832, a few weeks after the Reform Act became law. He left his body to the Webb Street School of Anatomy so that students could dissect

Jeremy Bentham, aged 75

Sir Edwin Chadwick

it to learn more about the way in which human bodies work. In the last few years of his life, Bentham employed Edwin Chadwick as his secretary. The two became close friends, and Bentham's influence on Chadwick was to have profound consequences.

Edwin Chadwick (1800–90)

Edwin Chadwick was born in 1800 just outside Manchester in a village called Longsight. Following the death of his mother and the failure of his father's business, Edwin Chadwick's family moved to London. His father became a journalist, and by 1812 had remarried and had become editor of the magazine the *New Statesman*. Four years later, Chadwick's father was offered the job of editor of the *Western Times*, and the family moved to Devon. Edwin did not go with them. He had decided to become a lawyer, and trained first as an attorney and then as a barrister. Both trainings were long and difficult.

By 1828 Edwin Chadwick was a struggling law student, who took on part-time newspaper work in order to help pay for his studies. He made a small income for himself by writing articles for *The Times* newspaper, and for journals like the *Westminster Review*. Work for his articles took him into the London slums, where he saw first hand the terrible conditions in which the poor lived. He met, too, Dr. Arnott and Dr. Southwood-Smith, who were to become his life-long friends. They took him to the worst fever hospitals. All this made him determined to work for improvements in the way in which the poorest people lived.

At about this time, he was introduced to Jeremy Bentham and to his friends, the Utilitarians. They all thought, talked and wrote a lot about the sorts of reform they would like to see introduced into Britain. The basis of all the reforms they discussed was the Principle of Utility – that of making sure that whatever was done increased the sum total of human happiness. Within a few weeks, Jeremy Bentham had invited Edwin Chadwick to work for him as his secretary, and Chadwick had moved into his home. They became firm friends, and worked together closely. Indeed, it was

Edwin Chadwick who nursed Jeremy Bentham through his last illness, and was with him when he died in April 1832.

The time spent with Jeremy Bentham and the Utilitarians had a profound effect on Edwin Chadwick. It altered the whole way he looked at social reform. Jeremy Bentham had taught him three important things:

1. Whatever the problem, whether it was how to give relief to paupers, or how to improve living conditions in towns for the poor, it was important to begin with the problem itself. No notice was to be taken of old solutions and old approaches to the problem. Fresh thinking was needed.

2. Government action was essential if social reform was really to be of any use. In the early years of the nineteenth century, most people believed that men and women should be able to get on with their own lives without government interference. This approach, called 'laissez-faire', was all very well in theory, but in practice it meant that, for example, mill-owners could force their employers to work for very long hours, builders could put up houses without drains or running water, and an inefficient and expensive system of poor relief could continue. Edwin Chadwick came to see that this kind of freedom could harm a lot of people and, eventually, the whole country. It was essential that the government should intervene.

3. Absolutely everything had to be judged by the Principle of Utility. Reforms were only good reforms if they increased the sum total of human happiness.

As Jeremy Bentham lay dying, an invitation came to Edwin Chadwick asking him to join the Poor Law Commission. Parliament had agreed that a commission should be set up to enquire into the workings of the Poor Law, and to make recommendations for change. This was too good an opportunity to miss. Chadwick gave up all thoughts of becoming a lawyer. He joined the Commission, and spent the rest of his life working tirelessly to put Bentham's ideas into practice.

3

THE POOR

Two Nations

In 1845 the Tory MP for Maidstone, Benjamin Disraeli, published a novel called *Sybil* or *The Two Nations*. Later, Disraeli was to become Prime Minister, but in 1845 he was an MP with a reputation for harrying his own leader, Robert Peel, in the House of Commons.

An advertisement for the book said that it was aimed at illustrating 'The Condition of the People'. The story told of a queen who reigns over:

'. . . Two nations; between whom there is no intercourse and no sympathy; who are as ignorant of each other's habits, thoughts and feelings, as if they were dwellers in different zones, or inhabitants of different planets; who are formed by a different breeding, are fed by a different food, are ordered by different manners, and are not governed by the same laws.'

'You speak of –' said Egremont, hesitatingly, 'THE RICH AND THE POOR.'

Most of the people who read *Sybil* knew that Disraeli was really writing about Great Britain. There were many writers who wanted their comfortable readers to know that there was another England about which they knew very little – whose people lived in the back streets and alleys of London, and in the new industrial towns and cities of the midlands and the north. Henry Mayhew, for example, wrote a series of articles in 1849–50 for the newspaper *The Morning Chronicle*, in which he described the many different patterns of life and work to be found among London's wage-earners. There were, of course, as Mayhew and other writers found out, many more divisions in society than simply 'the rich' and 'the poor'.

The Aristocracy

By the nineteenth century this term was used to describe about 300 of the very richest families. The dukes and earls, viscounts and barons who were the heads of these families sat in the House of Lords, and

A picture of a ballroom scene in the Illustrated London News *in May 1847*

many of them held important positions in the government. They also owned vast estates – normally about 10,000 acres each, as well as country mansions and houses in London.

In their country mansions the aristocracy lived on a grand scale. Each house was really a small community, with between forty and fifty indoor and outdoor servants to look after the needs of the owners. There would be, for example, gardeners, under-gardeners and grooms, valets and a butler, ladies maids, parlour maids and scullery maids, cooks and a housekeeper, and, if there were children in the family, a governess and nurse-maids.

Some families owned estates in more than one part of the country. The day-to-day running of these estates was left to bailiffs. This left the head of the family free to attend to local and national affairs. Their families moved from house to house according to the season. They might, for example, spend the grouse-shooting season in their Yorkshire house, the coldest parts of the winter in their Sussex house, and the fashionable 'season', when clothes were shown off and parties, dinners and balls attended, in their London house.

Not everyone approved of all of the parties which were held by the rich. William Taylor was a footman in 1837, and in his diary he described one party which was held in the house in which he worked:

'May 18
This is a very buisy day as we are going to have a party this evening something larger than usual. We had four to dinner and about fifty or sixty in the evening . . . The company comes generally about ten or eleven o'clock and stays until one or two in the morning. Sweet hearting matches are very often made up at these parties. Its quite disgusting to a modist eye to see the way the young ladies dress to atract the notice of the gentlemen. They are nearly naked to the waist, only just a little bit of dress hanging on the shoulder . . . Plenty of false haire and teeth and paint. If a person wish to see the way of the world, they must be a gentleman's servant, then they mite see it to perfection.'

The Gentry

The country gentry were also landowners, but not on such a large scale as the aristocracy. They generally owned estates of 1,000–3,000 acres, and usually lived in a comfortable house surrounded by gardens, with a home farm which was managed by a steward or bailiff. The rest of their estate was let out to tenant farmers, who paid rent. Few country gentlemen could afford to keep a house in London as well, and so they spent most of their time living on their estates. An American

This picture, 'Visiting the Poor' was printed in a book called **The Women of England** *which was written by Sarah Stickney Ellis and published in 1839*

girl, Anna Maria Fay, visited her uncle on his estate at Moor Park, Shropshire, in 1851. In one of her letters home she wrote:

'We rise early at half-past seven, have prayers at half-past eight, and breakfast a quarter of an hour later. After breakfast the children go to their schoolroom and Maria gives Kitty a music lesson. Aunt Catherine and I write or sew until eleven or twelve, when we go out driving. Uncle Richard either goes shooting by himself or with Mr Betton, and sometimes with Sir Charles Cuyler. We lunch when we return, and at six we dine. In the evening we form a very cheerful party by the drawing-room fire, reading, or sewing, or playing games with the children.'

A landed gentleman did not have to work to earn his living. The interest payments from his investments and the rents from his estates provided his income. Some invested money in industrial concerns to increase their income. Thomas Assheton Smith, for example, the squire of Tedworth in Hampshire, owned slate quarries in North Wales which paid him large sums of money each year.

Life for the landed gentry was not all hunting, shooting and fishing. Many of them took their local responsibilities very seriously. The women would visit poor, sick and needy people living on their family's estates and in nearby villages, and often did what they could to help them.

The men became magistrates, Guardians of the Poor and officers in the local yeomanry, and had a good deal of power and influence within a local neighbourhood.

The Middle Class

There has been, for hundreds of years, a group of people who were neither aristocracy nor gentry, and most certainly could not be called the 'labouring poor'. By 1692 these men and women were being called people of the 'middling sort'. By 1850 their numbers had grown considerably and they were being called, by some politicians, writers and speakers, the 'middle class'. This 'middle class' consisted of men and women with an enormously wide range of jobs and incomes, yet they all had one thing in common. They did not have to earn their living by manual labour.

The bankers and merchants of London, the coal and

In 1849 Alexis Soyer wrote a book called The Modern Housewife or Ménagère. *This is one of the illustrations in the book, and shows a middle-class family enjoying their Christmas dinner*

The Children who have cunningly reserved their infantine appetites for the grand national dish, the Blazing Plum Pudding.

iron masters of South Wales, the mill owners of Lancashire and Yorkshire, and the shipyard owners of Liverpool and Scotland were all very wealthy men. They lived with their families in large, comfortable houses with servants to care for them. Their way of life was almost the same as some of the aristocracy and gentry. Indeed, their sons and daughters often married the sons and daughters of wealthy, titled landowners. Many of the wealthy members of the middle class had worked their way up from very simple beginnings. Some became closely involved in the business life of the towns in which they worked. Not only did they employ large work forces, but they invested enormous sums of money in their own enterprises and the enterprises of others. They controlled the business life, and therefore the prosperity, of the cities in which they lived and worked.

There were also the doctors and lawyers who had had a university education and professional training. Some, like John Roberton, a Manchester surgeon (see page 64), worked amongst the navvies who built railway lines; others would earn a great deal more treating the families of the wealthy. All, however, would have been considered by those living at the time to have been middle class.

The vast majority of middle-class people were not, however, wealthy tycoons or trained professionals. They were shopkeepers and commercial travellers, teachers and railway guards, post-office clerks and coal merchants. Some of these were the people who had been given the vote by the 1832 Reform Act. Many of them earned less than the better paid members of the working classes. A school teacher, for example, might earn £60 a year compared to a cabinet maker's £100. Yet the cabinet maker, because he earned money by working with his hands, could never be considered a member of the middle class.

In the 1830s and 1840s many books were published about housekeeping. They were intended for the middle classes who could afford few, if any, servants. In 1849, for example, Alexis Soyer, a French chef, published a series of weekly menus suitable for middle-class people on different incomes. He suggested that a small shopkeeper and his wife, just setting out in business, might have roast beef, potatoes, greens and Yorkshire pudding for their Sunday dinner. When the shopkeeper had become prosperous, the family's Sunday dinner would consist of 'Pot au Feu, Fish – Haunch of Mutton, or a quarter of Lamb, or other good joint – Two Vegetables – Pastry and a Fruit Pudding – a little Dessert.'

Girls from middle-class families were expected to marry. If they did not, they usually remained in their parents' home, or went to live with a married brother or sister. Once married, a middle-class woman did not go out to work. She and her children were entirely dependent upon her husband's income. Indeed, everything she possessed legally belonged to him. For some women this was too restricting. Florence Nightingale, herself from a middle-class family, refused an offer of marriage. Writing in 1851, she said:

'Women don't consider themselves as human beings at all, there is absolutely no God, no country, no duty to them at all, except family.'

The Labouring Poor: 'those who will work'

Henry Mayhew divided the 'labouring poor' into 'those who will work, those who cannot work and those who will not work'. Mayhew found that the group he called 'those who will work' undertook an enormous range and variety of jobs. The work was invariably manual, which earned them the label 'labouring' or 'working' class, but not all of it was badly paid.

Skilled Artisans

The small group of highly skilled artisans – cabinet makers, jewellers and watchmakers, scientific instrument makers, breeches makers and hatters – could expect to earn between thirty shillings and forty shillings a week. These trades, however, were generally found in London. In the new iron, engineering and textile industries of the midlands and the north there were also workers who could afford a similar standard of living. These were the engineers at coal mines and in machine-tool workshops, the most skilled people in iron foundries and some foremen and supervisors in textile factories.

The next group of working people earned between twenty shillings and thirty shillings a week. They included building trade craftsmen, mule spinners and iron workers. Some had to look for work away from home: masons and bricklayers often tramped miles to get work, and so did those leading gangs of men on railway building contracts. The important point about all of this work is that it was regular.

Labourers

Carrying, lifting, dragging, digging, trenching, blasting, reaping, mowing, washing, scrubbing, sweeping and a thousand and one other jobs had to be done by hand. The work was hard, boring and sometimes dangerous. It had to be done in the pouring rain, the freezing snow and in the blazing sun, and it was invariably poorly paid. All industries employed men (and often women) to do this hard manual labour.

Navvies, originally builders of canals, but by the middle of the nineteenth century builders of railways, were regarded as the kings of labourers. Their work was strenuous and dangerous. In a good year a pickman and a shoveller could earn as much as twenty-four shillings a week; in bad times their wage could fall as low as fifteen shillings. Coalminers' work was often as dangerous as that of the navvies. Their wages varied from district to district, but generally between 1830 and 1850 a weekly wage of from fifteen shillings to twenty-five shillings was about average for a good year.

In 1851 there were over 1 million agricultural labourers who, together with 364,000 indoor farm servants, made up a work-force of about 1.5 million.

Lymington Ironworks in Northumberland

About half of all farms were worked by the farmer and his immediate family. The rest employed labourers for all or part of a year. Some of the regular labourers were expected to have some kind of special knowledge – as shepherds or ploughmen, for example. However, most agricultural labourers were expected to turn their hands to whatever farm work was to be done. Farm labourers in the north tended to earn more than those in the south: about fourteen shillings per week would be paid to labourers in the West Riding, but seven shillings in Gloucestershire, Wiltshire and Suffolk. Sometimes a cottage went with the job.

Town labourers were much less of a single, clearly defined group than the navvies, miners or agricultural labourers. They were the dock-workers, the carters, the sweepers, the porters, and the labourers in the brickyards, ironworks and breweries. They could never be sure from day to day whether they would get work. They were paid by the day or by the week, and were laid off as soon as there was no work to do. In good times, if they were healthy and strong enough, there would be work for most of the year. In bad times, like the 1830s and 1840s, few worked for any length of time, and lived on the edge of starvation.

The Labouring Poor: 'those who cannot work'

For much of the year there was simply no work for labourers. Some, such as bricklayers, street-sellers and house-painters, could only work when the weather was fine. Others, such as hat-makers and tailors, tended to have a lot of work between February and July, but nothing very much for the rest of the year. Similarly when trade was bad, for example in 1831, 1837, 1841–2, and 1847–8, thousands of workers were laid off. There was no redundancy money and no unemployment benefit. Only the skilled artisans might have been able to put by enough money to live on for a short period of time until work picked up again. The others had to make do as best they could. Some took what few possessions they had to the local pawn-broker and got a little money that way; others relied on the goodwill of local shopkeepers to give them credit; many begged in the streets; most existed on a near-starvation diet of bread, potatoes and tea.

For those who were sick or injured, life was a hand-to-mouth existence. Many accidents happened at work. Navvying and mining could mean broken and smashed bones, and torn ligaments and muscles were common. Agricultural labourers faced long hours of heavy work in all weathers. A poor diet, wet clothing and damp cottages made bronchitis, pneumonia, tuberculosis and arthritis common. Workers in factories and mills faced dangers from unfenced machinery. Scalps were torn off when hair became caught, fingers were crushed, and arms and legs broken. Occasionally an employer might make some small payment by way of recompense. Injury or illness to one or more members of a family meant that the whole family suffered.

The Illustrated London News *published this drawing of a hay-harvest in August 1846*

The old had neither the strength nor the health to work. There were no state pensions or supplementary benefits. The best that an elderly person could hope for was that a child, or other relative, would look after them until they died. Those for whom this was not possible faced a very grim old age.

The Labouring Poor: 'those who will not work'

Beggars and Vagrants

Vagrants in tattered clothes tramping the roads between village, town and city were a common sight in nineteenth-century Britain. Henry Mayhew noted that they were almost always men or boys, and were usually aged between fifteen and twenty-five. Some may well have started out as unemployed labourers, tramping from town to town looking for work. By the time they had become vagrants, they had no intention of looking for work, but simply wandered from place to place, begging when they needed food. It was, of course, almost impossible to count them, but Mayhew estimated that there were some 40,000–100,000 destitute men and boys tramping around Great Britain.

Beggars were a common sight in all towns and cities. Many had a 'patch' which they worked, keeping to certain streets and squares. Some claimed to have been sailors or soldiers, machine operatives or gentlemen fallen on hard times. Anything, in fact, which would force the conscience of passers-by to give them some money.

Pick-pockets and Burglars

Pick-pocketing, petty theft, house-breaking and burglary were all common in Britain in the nineteenth century. Those prepared to risk prison and possible transportation could 'earn' enough to live on. Some of this petty crime was well organised, with young boys being apprenticed to gangs, and taught their 'trade' in stages by experienced and successful thieves.

All the labouring poor, whether they were breeches-makers or dock-workers, street-cleaners or factory operatives, relied upon their own physical strength and fitness for their wages. Invariably these wages were low. When a labourer's health failed, or when trade was bad, he might try another occupation. If he found no work at all, he and his family might have no alternative but to turn to the parish for help.

The Poor Law System before 1834

In 1815 there was a way of providing official help for the poor who could not support themselves. The framework of this system had been set up by the Elizabethan Poor Law of 1601. This framework had remained, in spite of the tremendous changes which had taken place in the countryside and in the towns. It had remained unchanged partly because it was so flexible that it could be adapted to suit different local conditions, and partly because it was accepted by those who had to pay for it.

Overseers

Each parish was responsible for its own people. All property owners paid a poor-rate which was collected by the Overseer of the Poor, who was appointed by the local magistrates. He was usually unpaid, and was a rate-payer himself. In most parishes the more important rate-payers took it in turns to be overseer. It was the overseer's responsibility to help, or 'give relief', to the poor. Not all overseers were kind, generous men. Many did their best, but some were corrupt and not all the money they collected reached the poor. Others put their own interests first by keeping the poor-rate as low as possible. The poor in these parishes were badly treated when compared with parishes where the magistrates appointed good overseers who collected a reasonable rate and used it well.

Paupers

Men, women and children who received regular help (relief) from their parish were called paupers. Those who could not work – the impotent poor – were the old, widows, children, ill, injured and handicapped, and women with young children to support. They were usually given small sums of money to help them through difficult times. For paupers who were ill, the overseer usually paid a local doctor a fee for looking after them. Pauper children were sent to be trained in a local trade.

The paupers who could work, but either could not or would not find work, caused the authorities great problems. They were often very poor indeed, and clearly needed help of some kind. However, because they were actually able to work (unlike the impotent poor) the parish authorities took a very different attitude to them. The overseer would always try to find work of some kind for them to do in exchange for the relief which they received.

Settlement

Many people moved from parish to parish in search of work. Often the parish in which they were living when they were finally forced to ask for relief was not the one in which they were born, or the one in which they had been married. In 1662 Parliament passed a Settlement Act which allowed overseers to send paupers back to their own parish to get relief. A person had 'settlement' in a parish if he or she had been born there, had worked there for a year or more, had moved there to start an apprenticeship, or had lived there in property worth £10 a year or more. Married women automatically took their husband's place of settlement.

People were, of course, allowed to move out of their parish to work elsewhere. They took with them a 'Certificate of Settlement' which stated that their own parish would be responsible for them if they ever needed relief. However, certificates were lost, or forgotten, or never asked for in the first place. If a man or woman needed relief whilst they were living away from their home parish, they had to go before a magistrate and answer questions about their family background and the work they had done. The magistrate would then decide which parish should pay relief – and in which parish they should live. There were often fierce arguments between parishes. Paupers could be shunted backwards and forwards between several parishes, with all the overseers concerned being equally determined not to give them settlement, and therefore relief, in their particular parish.

Workhouses

The able-bodied paupers were a problem for the overseers. Most needed relief because they could not find work to do, but overseers could only give relief for work done. So jobs had to be created. An Act of Parliament of 1723 said that parishes could, if they wanted to, build workhouses for the able-bodied poor. They were equipped with looms and tools, and the paupers could make goods to sell. Parishes were allowed to refuse to give relief to able-bodied paupers who would not enter a workhouse. By 1776 there were almost 2,000 of these 'Poorhouses' or 'Houses of Industry' in England. Some were light and airy, and really did help the poor. Others were filthy, sordid dens of misery.

Gilbert's Act, passed in 1782, changed all this. Parishes were allowed to group together to build a workhouse. However, one of the most important clauses in the Act stated that these workhouses were to be used only for the impotent poor – the ill, the old, mothers with children and children by themselves. All paupers who were capable of working should be given relief outside the workhouse.

The Roundsman System and the Labour-Rate

Providing work for able-bodied paupers inside a workhouse was one thing. Finding work for them outside, in the parish, was quite another. Often there was no work to be had, and the overseers had to be quite inventive.

One system which was widely used was the 'Roundsman system'. The parish overseer would give a pauper a 'ticket' which he, or she, would take round

Parish workhouse of St. James' London, 1809. How are the paupers being helped?

to all the local farmers and other employers. If there was a job to be done, the pauper would hand over the 'ticket'. The employer would then pay the pauper a wage which matched exactly that which the parish would have paid in poor relief.

In some areas, the parish itself created work for able-bodied paupers. When the work was done, the parish 'paid' the paupers with relief.

Other parishes used a system called the 'Labour-Rate'. Rate-payers had to pay both a poor-rate and a labour-rate. The money collected from the labour-rate was put into a fund from which paupers were paid when they worked for the parish. Employers could, if they wanted to, opt out of the labour-rate. If they did this, they had to guarantee to employ a certain number of paupers, and pay them for the work which they did.

The Allowance System

Many people who were in work were still too poor to support their families. Many parishes tried to give relief to poor people according to their needs, not according to the work which they had done. This meant that the Overseer had to take into consideration such things as

the size of the pauper's family.

Some parishes, like Winfarthing in Norfolk, used a very simple system to work out relief:

The Winfarthing system of relief

Income should be	For a Man	For a Single Woman	For a Man and Wife	With 1 Child	With 2 Children
When the gallon loaf is 1s 0d	3s 0d	2s 0d	4s 6d	6s 0d	7s 6d
When the gallon loaf is 1s 1d	3s 3d	2s 1d	4s 10d	6s 5d	8s 0d
When the gallon loaf is 1s 2d	3s 6d	2s 2d	5s 2d	6s 10d	8s 6d
When the gallon loaf is 1s 3d	3s 9d	2s 3d	5s 6d	7s 3d	9s 0d
When the gallon loaf is 1s 4d	4s 0d	2s 4d	5s 10d	7s 8d	9s 6d
When the gallon loaf is 1s 5d	4s 0d	2s 5d	5s 11d	7s 10d	9s 9d
When the gallon loaf is 1s 6d	4s 3d	2s 6d	6s 3d	8s 3d	10s 3d
When the gallon loaf is 1s 7d	4s 3d	2s 7d	6s 4d	8s 5d	10s 6d
When the gallon loaf is 1s 8d	4s 6d	2s 8d	6s 8d	8s 10d	11s 0d
When the gallon loaf is 1s 9d	4s 6d	2s 9d	6s 9d	9s 0d	11s 3d
When the gallon loaf is 1s 10d	4s 9d	2s 10d	7s 1d	9s 5d	11s 9d

Loaf weighing 8 lb 11 oz

The Speenhamland system

Other parishes, such as Speenhamland in Berkshire, operated a very complicated system of relief. This based relief not only on the size of a pauper's family, but also on the price of bread.

By the beginning of the nineteenth century, the system of giving relief to the poor was stretched to breaking point. It had never been designed to cope with the results of the changes in the countryside. Cities and towns were growing at a rapid rate, and were often only covered by one or two parishes. A bad year for trade or for industry would mean that thousands of people might be wanting to claim poor relief at the same time and from the same parish.

The number of poor and destitute people was increasing year by year, and so was the cost of supporting them. Between 1783 and 1785 the average expenditure on poor relief had been £2,004,000. By 1829–33 this had risen to £6,758,000. Rate-payers felt the burden was too high; for the poor this was not enough.

The Collapse of the Old Poor Law System

Corn Laws and the Price of Bread

The war with France (1793–1815) had made British arable farmers very prosperous. In 1806 the French Emperor Napoleon ordered his ships to prevent any trade between Britain and Europe. This blockade meant that no foreign corn could be imported into Britain, which in turn meant that farmers could charge high prices for their British corn. The blockade lasted for three years, but the war continued until 1815, and trade was disrupted for a long time. The difficulty of importing foreign corn and a series of bad harvests meant that British farmers were able to profit by keeping their corn prices high. But high corn prices meant high bread prices. Even though there was plenty of work and wages were rising fast, the cost of food and other goods was rising even faster. An increasing number of people had to ask their parishes for relief.

The end of the war with France in 1815 brought no improvement. The harvests of 1813 and 1814 had been good in England and on the continent. Cheap foreign corn could once more be imported from Europe, which forced the British farmers to keep their prices low. They had war-time taxes to pay as well as large increases in the poor-rate, and interest on loans raised to cover the cost of enclosure. Many went bankrupt, which could mean unemployment for their labourers. Farmers who survived were forced to reduce the wages they paid to their workers. Those whom they employed were pushed closer to the workhouse. The already creaking structure of the old Poor Law was close to collapse.

In 1815 Members of Parliament tried to improve the situation. They passed the Corn Law, which said that foreign corn could not be imported until the cost of British corn was as high as eighty shillings a quarter. Parliament hoped that this would hold the price of corn steady, and therefore the price of bread would remain steady as well. This, in turn, should mean that, because the landowners' profits would not go wildly up and down as they had done in the immediate past, the wages which the farmers paid to their labourers would remain stable as well.

It did not quite work out like this. Many people, both employed and unemployed, resented the Corn Law. They believed it kept the price of corn, and therefore of bread, unnecessarily high. There were riots and outbreaks of violence up and down the country.

Captain Swing

It was not only the poor who felt the consequences of greater poverty. More paupers meant higher poor-rates, and many rate-payers began to object. In the 1820s many parishes actually reduced the allowances they paid to paupers. Parishes which had used a sliding scale relating to bread prices, such as the Speenhamland system, began ignoring the price of bread, and simply paid a flat rate based upon the number of children in a family. Even labourers' families who did not receive parish relief had barely enough to live on.

William Cobbett, riding towards Warminster, Wiltshire, on 31st August 1826 reported that:

'The labourers here look as if they were half
starved . . . For my own part, I really am ashamed
to ride a fat horse, to have a full belly, and to
have a clean shirt upon my back when I look at
these wretched countrymen of mine; while I
actually see them reeling with weakness; when I
see their poor faces present me with nothing but
skin and bone . . .'

Many farmers in the south and east of Britain had
introduced threshing machines. These could do the
work of several men, and took away winter employment. Labourers who feared starvation burned hay-
ricks and destroyed threshing machines. They had little
chance of finding any other employment. Farmers were
sent threatening notes signed by 'Captain Swing':

> Sir
>
> This is to acquaint you
> that if your thrashing Ma-
> chines are not destroyed by
> you directly we shall com-
> mence our labours
>
> signed on behalf
> of the whole
> Swing

These notes gave the impression of a general, organised movement. In fact there was no 'Captain
Swing'. Local bands of desperate labourers all used
the same name simply to add to what they hoped was
the fear which would be felt by the farmers. Some
farmers attempted to agree terms with the Swing
rioters before their own crops or property were
destroyed; all farmers condemned 'Captain Swing'.

Poverty in the Towns

The ending of the wars with France brought problems
for the manufacturers as well as for the farmers. There
was no longer any need for the vast quantities of iron
and textiles which had equipped and clothed the troops
fighting abroad. In 1815 manufacturers found new
markets for both iron and textiles in America and, once
trade with the continent was possible, in Europe. Soon
both America and Europe were full of British products.
Prices dropped, and continental manufacturers began
to persuade their governments to prevent British goods
being imported. Within three years British exports
dropped by a third and there was unemployment in
factories, mills and workshops.

This illustration, 'The Home of the Rick Burner', was
published in the satirical magazine Punch in 1844. Was
the artist in sympathy with the rick burners, or not?

In the manufacturing districts there was an unemployment problem which went on beyond the years
immediately after the war. The great northern industrial towns like Bradford and Manchester, with their
woollen and cotton mills, provided jobs for people who
lived in the area. But mill work was often available only
at certain times of the year. This was because fashions
could change and the demand for certain kinds of
cloth could lessen, or the cotton crop could fail, or the
wool from one year's shearing could be of a poor
quality. Large numbers of workers would be laid off
and would ask for poor relief. For many months the
overseers would have merely routine requests for relief
to deal with. Then suddenly they would be swamped
with thousands of requests for help.

Added to this was the distress of some workers, like
the hand-loom weavers, who had been responsible and
respectable members of society, earning a good wage.
Once machinery could make cloth, their particular skills
were no longer wanted. Some found work in mills and
workshops; others had to accept greatly lowered wages
and were closer than ever they had been to needing
parish relief.

Some workers, in times of particular hardship,
blamed the machinery itself. They saw machines as
taking jobs away from people. These people turned to
destruction and machine breaking as a solution.

For all these different reasons, pressure was put on
the Poor Law system as more and more workers applied
for relief. The old structure, designed for mainly rural
areas, simply could not cope.

SOURCE WORK:
The collapse of the Old Poor Law

1. Parishes used different ways of helping the poor before 1834. Two of these ways were the Allowance system (look back at page 45) and the Roundsman system (look back at page 44).
   (a) What were the advantages of each of these systems for (i) farmers, and (ii) paupers ?
   (b) What were the disadvantages of each of these systems for (i) farmers, and (ii) paupers ?

SOURCE A

A notice issued by Berkshire magistrates, November 1830:

TO THE

Labouring Classes

— ✦ —

THE Gentlemen, Yeomanry, Farmers, and others, having made known to you their intention of increasing your **Wages** to a satisfactory extent; and it having been resolved that **Threshing Machines** shall not be again used; it is referred to your good Sense that it will be most beneficial to your own permanent Interests to return to your usual honest occupations, and to withdraw yourselves from practices which tend to destroy the Property from whence the very means of your additional **Wages** are to be supplied.

Hungerford, 22nd November, 1830.

EMBERLIN AND HAROLD, PRINTERS, BOOKSELLERS, DRUGGISTS, &c. STAMP-OFFICE, MARLBOROUGH.

---

2. Read the Notice issued by the Berkshire magistrates in November 1830.
   (a) What did the farmers promise to do about (i) wages, and (ii) threshing machines?
   (b) What hidden threat do the magistrates make in this notice?
   (c) How might a farmer have explained why he agreed to this notice being put up?
   (d) How might a farm labourer have reacted to this notice?
   Use your own knowledge and understanding to explain your answers.

SOURCE B

Annual average wheat prices in England and Wales 1801–1850:

Period	Highest Price	Lowest Price
1801–05	119s 6d	62s 3d
1806–10	106s 5d	75s 4d
1811–15	126s 6d	65s 7d
1816–20	96s 11d	67s 7d
1821–25	66s 6d	44s 7d
1826–30	66s 3d	58s 6d
1831–35	66s 4d	39s 4d
1836–40	70s 8d	48s 6d
1841–45	64s 4d	50s 1d
1846–50	69s 9d	40s 3d

(From *Captain Swing*, Hobsbawm and Rudé, Lawrence and Wishart, 1969)

SOURCE C

Wages of a hand-loom weaver in Bolton:

1797	1800	1805	1810	1816	1820	1824	1830
30s	25s	25s	19s	12s	9s	8s 6d	5s 6d

(From *Plenty and Want*, John Burnett, Thomas Nelson, 1966)

3. (a) Look at Source C. How does this source, together with Source B, help to explain the rising cost of poor relief?
   (b) What other reasons were there for the rising cost of poor relief? (You will need to look back at pages 46–7 to help you explain your answer.)

4. Was the rising cost of poor relief the only reason that changes were needed to the Poor Law?

The Poor Law Amendment Act, 1834

The Poor Law Commission, 1832–4

'We, the Commissioners appointed by Your Majesty to make a diligent and full inquiry into the practical operation of the Laws for the Relief of the Poor in England and Wales, and into the manner in which those laws are administered, and to report our opinion whether any and what alterations, amendments, or improvements may be beneficially made in the said laws . . .'

The *Report of Commissioners into the Administration and Operation of the Laws for the Relief of the Poor* begins with these phrases. They describe in detail what they had been asked to do. Who had set up this Commission and given it these instructions?

The government had decided to discover in detail how the system of poor relief was working, and how it could be improved. They therefore set up a Commission to discover these things. They appointed eight Commissioners and twenty-six Assistant Commissioners to carry out a detailed enquiry into the working of the Poor Law. However, even before they set out, the Commissioners knew what they hoped would be found. First, that the Poor Law system was itself a cause of poverty. Whenever it gave outdoor relief, such as helping to make up a labourer's wages, it encouraged them to be idle. They would not start to find work which would pay enough to support their families. Second, the Commissioners hoped to find that the way in which the Poor Law was run by the local overseers and magistrates was inefficient. The only solution would be for central government to supervise a system for the whole country.

The Assistant Commissioners visited around 3,000 parishes and produced a mass of information which together formed the *Poor Law Report* of 1834. The reports which came in from the parishes showed that the system of giving relief to the poor was both inefficient and corrupt. Workhouses, like the one shown on page 45, were criticised for providing a soft life for their inmates. Other workhouses were found to be wasteful and inefficient. Some overseers were corrupt:

'As a body, I found annual overseers wholly incompetent to discharge the duties of their office . . . Their object is to get through the year with as little unpopularity and trouble as possible, their successors, therefore, have frequently to complain of demands left unsettled, and rates uncollected, either from carelessness or a desire to gain the trifling popularity of having called for fewer assessments than usual . . .'

(From the *Poor Law Report*, 1834)

Above all, the Assistant Commissioners reported that it was the system of outdoor relief which was the most inefficient and wasteful of all:

'The great source of abuse is outdoor relief as afforded to the able-bodied.'

(From the *Poor Law Report*, 1834)

The Commission produced a detailed report in 1834. It was largely the work of Nassau Senior, one of the Commissioners, and Edwin Chadwick, a hardworking Assistant Commissioner who had been promoted to Commissioner.

What did the Poor Law Report recommend?

It recommended, not surprisingly, the ending of outdoor relief for the able-bodied poor:

'Except as to medical attention . . . all relief whatever to able bodied persons or to their families, otherwise than in well regulated workhouses . . . shall be declared unlawful and shall cease.'

All those who were capable of working, should work. If able-bodied people could not find work, then they and their families had to enter a workhouse. The Report recognised that there were some people – the old, the sick, the handicapped, widows and orphan children – who genuinely could not look after themselves. They had to be cared for in a workhouse. Yet at the same time, workhouses had to be made fairly grim places so that the able-bodied poor would not be tempted to give up work and go and live in them. Conditions inside the workhouse had to be worse than the conditions of the poorest labourer outside the workhouse:

'The first and essential of all conditions . . . is that his [*the pauper's*] situation on the whole shall not be made really or apparently so eligible as the situation of the independent labourer of the lowest class.'

Once in the workhouse, separation was necessary:

'At least four classes are necessary:
(1) The aged and really impotent
(2) The children
(3) The able-bodied females
(4) The able-bodied males . . .'

The Report suggested that parishes should be grouped into Unions, and the building of one Union workhouse big enough for all the paupers in the district. Each Union would have a Board of Guardians of the Poor, elected by the rate-payers. This Board of Guardians would be guided by the Poor Law Commissioners who would operate from London, controlling the system and enforcing regulations.

The Poor Law Amendment Act, 1834

The government acted quickly. In August 1834 the Poor Law Amendment Act became law. Many, but not all of the recommendations of the *Poor Law Report* were put into the Act.

A cartoon published in 1836, two years after the Poor Law Amendment became Law. What was the cartoonist's attitude to the old Poor Law and to the new Poor Law?

A central Poor Law Commission was set up in London to administer poor relief throughout the country. Three paid Commissioners were appointed to introduce and supervise the system. The Chairman was Thomas Frankland Lewis, who had been a Tory MP. The other two Commissioners were George Nicholls, who had once been a workhouse overseer, and John Shaw Lefevre, a lawyer. Edwin Chadwick was appointed full-time Secretary to the Commission. The job of these four men was to advise and guide the Poor Law officers throughout the country. However, it was Chadwick, with his hatred of waste and his love of efficiency, who had the greatest influence on the way in which the new Poor Law was put into operation.

What Parliament tried to do was to set up the basic structure of the new Poor Law. It did *not* try to lay down a series of detailed rules.

Parishes were to be grouped into Unions. The ratepayers living in each Union of parishes elected a Board of Guardians by open, not secret, ballot. This Board of Guardians was responsible for the way in which poor relief was organised and run within their own particular Union. Poor-rates were still collected by each Union of parishes, and used in that Union for the relief of poverty. Each Union had to build a workhouse – or adapt an existing one.

Each Poor Law Union appointed officials, some full-time and some part-time, to see that the Poor Law was administered correctly and the workhouse was run properly. The most important officer was the Clerk, whose job it was to make sure that the wishes of the Board of Guardians were carried out. The Medical Of-

ficer, usually an underpaid local doctor willing to take on the work for low pay, cared for sick paupers whether they were in the workhouse or receiving outdoor relief in their own homes. Outdoor relief was organised by the Relieving Officer, who would bring into the workhouse those who were too sick or frail to manage by themselves. The workhouse had a Master and a Matron who usually lived in, and who were responsible for the day-to-day running of the 'House'. Some officials were hard working and honest people who did their best for the paupers in their care. Others were corrupt, and did their best to make as much as they could from the system.

Although detailed rules as to how the poor were to be given relief were not laid down by Parliament, it was clear that Parliament expected the Unions of parishes to follow the recommendations of the *Poor Law Report*. It was quite clear that Parliament intended there to be one national system of poor relief. It was also clear that the basis of this poor relief was to be the workhouse. The Poor Law Amendment Act did not, however, forbid outdoor relief. The *Poor Law Report* hoped that it would. But Parliament was much more cautious and the Act stated:

'. . . it shall be lawful for the Commissioners, by such rules, orders or regulations as they think fit, to declare to what extent and for what period the relief to be given to able-bodied persons and their families in any particular parish or union may be administered out of the workhouse . . . by payments in money or with food or clothing . . .'

SOURCE WORK:
The New Poor Law – Buildings, Separation and Rules

SOURCE A

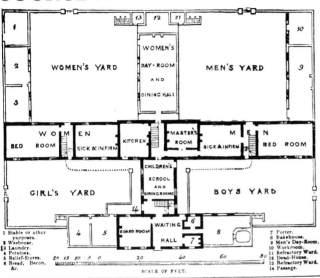

[K.]   No. 2. One Pair Plan.

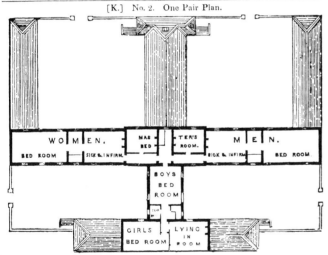

1. Source A is a plan of a workhouse. It was published by the Poor Law Commissioners to show Poor Law Guardians the type of workhouse which ought to be built.

   What does the plan tell you about the ways in which the Commissioners thought that: (i) men, (ii) women, (iii) boys, and (iv) girls should be treated?

SOURCE B

'Art. 9 The paupers, so far as the workhouse admits thereof, shall be classed as follows . . .
Class 1. Men infirm through age or any other cause.
Class 2. Able-bodied men, and youths above the age of 15 years.
Class 3. Boys above the age of 7 years, and under that of 15.
Class 4. Women infirm through age or any other cause.
Class 5. Able-bodied women, and girls above the age of 15.
Class 6. Girls above the age of 7 years, and under that of 15.
Class 7. Children under 7 years of age.'

(From the *First Report of the Poor Law Commissioners,* 1835)

2. The plan, together with Source B, can tell you something about the *attitudes* of the Poor Law Commissioners toward the paupers for whom they were responsible.

   Explain carefully, using Sources A and B, and your own knowledge, whether you agree or disagree with the following statements:

   (A) The Commissioners believed that people who were poor enough to need to go into a workhouse had no right to stay with their families, and so they split them up.

   (B) The Commissioners cared very much for the paupers for whom they were responsible, and so they encouraged Guardians to make sure that workhouses had their own laundry, bakehouse and school.

   (C) The Commissioners believed that the system of poor relief had to be as cheap and efficient as possible.

The New Poor Law

SOURCE C

AYLSHAM UNION.

WE THE POOR LAW COMMISSIONERS for England and Wales, do hereby Order and Direct, that the Paupers of the respective Classes and Sexes described in the Table hereunder written, who may be received and maintained in the Workhouse or Workhouses of the said Aylsham Union, shall, during the period of their residence therein, be fed, dieted, and maintained with the food and in the manner described and set forth in the said Table; viz.

Dietary for Able-bodied Men and Women.

		BREAKFAST		DINNER							SUPPER		
		Bread.	Milk Gruel.	Meat Pudding.	Potatoes or other Vegetables	Yeast Dumpling	Suet Pudding.	Bread.	Cheese.		Bread.	Cheese.	Butter.
		oz.	pint.	oz.	oz.	oz.	oz.	oz.	oz.		oz.	oz.	oz.
Sunday	Men	7	1	—	—	—	—	9	1		7	¾	---
	Women	5	1	—	—	—	—	8	1		5	---	½
Monday	Men	7	1	—	16	—	14	—	—		7	¾	---
	Women	5	1	—	12	—	12	—	—		5	---	½
Tuesday	Men	7	1	12	16	—	—	—	—		7	¾	---
	Women	5	1	10	12	—	—	—	—		5	---	½
Wednesday	Men	7	1	—	16	—	—	7	¾		7	¾	---
	Women	5	1	—	12	—	—	5	1½		5	---	½
Thursday	Men	7	1	12	16	—	—	—	—		7	¾	---
	Women	5	1	10	12	—	—	—	—		5	---	½
Friday	Men	7	1	—	16	—	—	7	¾		7	¾	---
	Women	5	1	—	12	—	—	5	½		5	---	½
Saturday	Men	7	1	—	16	11	—	—	—		7	¾	---
	Women	5	1	—	12	11	—	—	—		5	---	½

AND We do hereby further Order and Direct, that Children under the age of nine years, resident in the said Workhouse, shall be fed, dieted, and maintained with such food and in such manner as the said Guardians shall direct; and that Children above the age of nine years, and under the age of sixteen years, shall be allowed the same quantities as are prescribed in the above Table for able-bodied Women.

And We do also Order and Direct, that the sick paupers, resident in the said Workhouse, shall be fed, dieted, and maintained in such manner as the Medical Officer for the Workhouse shall direct.

And We do hereby further Order and Direct, that the Master or Masters of the Workhouse or Workhouses of the said Union shall cause two or more copies of this our Order, legibly written, or printed in a large type, to be hung up in the most public places of such Workhouse, and to renew the same from time to time, so that it be always kept fair and legible.

Given under our Hands and Seal of Office, this Second day of October, in the year One thousand eight hundred and forty-five.

(Signed)

GEO. NICHOLLS.
G. C. LEWIS.

CLEMENTS, PRINTER, MARKET-PLACE, AYLSHAM.

3. Read Source C.
   (a) What were the main differences between what men and women paupers in the Aylsham Union had to eat?
   (b) What reasons might the Guardians have had for making these differences?

The New Poor Law

SOURCE D

'WORKHOUSE (Rules of Conduct)

Any Pauper who shall neglect to observe any of the regulations therein contained as are applicable and binding on him:-

Or who shall make any noise when silence is ordered to be kept;
Or shall use obscene or profane language;
Or shall refuse or neglect to work, after having been required to do so;
Or shall play at cards or other games of chance;

Shall be deemed DISORDERLY.

Any pauper who shall within seven days, repeat any one or commit more than one of the offences specified . . .
Or shall by word or deed insult or revile the master or matron, or any other officer of the workhouse, or any of the Guardians,
Or shall be drunk;
Or shall wilfully disturb the other inmates during prayers or divine worship;

Shall be deemed REFACTORY.

It shall be lawful for the master of the workhouse . . . to punish any **disorderly** pauper by substituting, during a time not greater than forty-eight hours, for his or her dinner, . . . a meal consisting of eight ounces of bread, or one pound of cooked potatoes and also by witholding from him during the same period, all butter, cheese, tea, sugar, or broth. .

And it shall be lawful for the Board of Guardians . . . to order any **refactory** pauper to be punished by confinement to a separate room, with or without an alteration to the diet for no longer than twenty-four hours . . .'

(From the *Seventh Annual Reports of the Poor Law Commissioners*, 1841)

(Refractory = stubborn or obstinate)

4. Read these rules carefully.
   What can you learn from them about:
   (a) the way in which workhouses were run?
   (b) the way in which paupers behaved inside workhouses?

SOURCE E

'. . . if, for any special reason, it shall at any time appear to the Board of Guardians to be desirable to depart from the regulations in respect of any married couple, being paupers of the first and fourth classes (infirm men and infirm women), the Guardians shall be at liberty to resolve that such a couple shall have a sleeping apartment separate from those of other paupers . . . The master of the workhouse (subject to any regulations to be made by the Board of Guardians and approved by the Poor Law Commissioners) shall allow the father or mother of any child in the same workhouse to have an interview with such child at some one time in each day . . .
   . . . the Board of Guardians shall make arrangements for permitting the members of the same family who may be in different workhouses to have occasional interviews with each other, at such times and in such manner as may best suit the discipline of the several workhouses.'

(From the *Annual Reports of the Poor Law Commissioners*, 1835–41)

5. Read Source E carefully. Look back at Sources A and B, and at your answers to questions 1 and 2.
   Does Source E make you change your opinions about the Poor Law Commissioners?

6. Were the Poor Law Commissioners cruel to the paupers for whom they were responsible?

Opposition to the New Poor Law

The Commissioners did not waste any time in getting the Poor Law Unions organised. The actual work was carried out by the Assistant Commissioners, who began with the southern counties of England, which were mainly agricultural. In the first year after the Act was passed, 2,066 parishes were grouped into 112 Unions and Boards of Guardians were elected; in the second year, 5,800 parishes were grouped into 239 Unions. There was some opposition to what they were doing, as the Commissioners themselves stated in their annual report of 1836: 'The powers of the Act and our means of carrying it into operation', they wrote, 'have been put to the proof [test] by every means that ingenuity could devise.' This sort of opposition, the Commissioners believed, was to be expected. However, the Commissioners reported that many pauper labourers quickly understood the purpose of the new Poor Law, because in many districts they 'set themselves, without much delay, fairly and honestly to seek a livelihood by their own industry.'

This, however, was in the agricultural south. In the first half of the 1830s there was work to be found. There was some truth in the Commissioners' assumption that the poor could always find work if they were made to do so. At the beginning of 1837, when the Commissioners turned their attentions to the northern counties, they found a very different situation. A fall-off in trade meant that factories and mills had closed down. There was no work to be had.

Opposition in the North

There was a great deal of opposition in the north of England to the introduction of the new Poor Law. This section is about the experience of one town: the woollen mill town of Bradford in West Yorkshire. However, Bradford was only one of many northern industrial towns to fight against the introduction of the new Poor Law. A pattern of angry meetings, riots and disturbances was repeated over and over again across the north of England. People formed anti-Poor Law committees, held meetings, laid plans and printed and circulated emotional ballads and broadsides.

What really worried the Poor Law Commissioners was that the protesters were not just the poor – but mill-owners, shopkeepers and preachers as well. Richard Oastler, a Huddersfield mill-owner, Joseph Rayner Stephens, a non-conformist minister and John Fielden, a cotton manufacturer from Todmorden, led the opposition. They were agreed that a system which seemed to be going to put large numbers of paupers in workhouses for long periods of time simply wasn't suitable for the northern industrial towns. It was true that there would be unemployment, and large numbers of workers would be looking for relief. But this relief would be needed for short periods of time only, until trade picked up again. The new Poor Law, in their eyes, simply was not good for business. Neither was it making the best use of rate-payers' money to build and staff large workhouses which would stand half empty for most of the time.

A view of Bradford from the south-east, 1841

Bradford, West Yorkshire

In 1837 Bradford was a prosperous industrial town. The main industry was the production of worsted, which was a light, fine woollen cloth. The town was growing fast. In 1801 about 6,500 people lived in Bradford. By 1851 this had increased to 52,500. Of course, the main reason for this enormous increase was that people had been attracted to come and live and work in Bradford because there were jobs to be had and money to be made.

However, not everyone was employed for all of the time, and not everyone made money. Many men, women and children needed poor relief – but only for some months in the very bad years, and certainly not all the time. You read on page 47 of some of the problems of poverty in the northern industrial towns. Read this section again, and try to keep it in your mind as you find out now about the crisis facing Bradford in 1837.

The Riot Begins

On 30th October 1837 an angry crowd of about 300 people gathered outside the Court House in Bradford, West Yorkshire. They hurled abuse at the Poor Law Guardians, and jostled them as they pushed their way through to a meeting. The meeting was important. It was between the Guardians and Alfred Power. Mr Power was one of the Assistant Commissioners from the Central Poor Law Commission in London, and he had come to give the Guardians advice about bringing in the new Poor Law.

The Guardians were determined to hold their private meeting with Mr Power. The mob were equally determined that they would not. Each time a Guardian entered the Court House, a section of the crowd rushed the door. If a meeting was to be held, then some townspeople were going to be there and their views were going to be made known! However, they were told that the meeting was a private one, and there was not the slightest chance of any of them being allowed in. This enraged the crowd; they jostled and pushed the doors, shouting and arguing. They made so much noise that the Guardians were worried that they would not be able to get through their meeting without ugly scenes. They decided, unanimously, to move secretly to the nearby Sun Inn.

A Hostile Meeting

Matthew Thompson, one of the Guardians, arrived late. He was horrified to find that the meeting had been moved to the Sun Inn. He told the Guardians that this would only give the impression that they had something to hide. He persuaded his fellow Guardians to move back to a larger room in the Court House and to open the meeting to the public. This they did. The public gallery was quickly filled with members of the waiting crowd, by now angry and suspicious.

The crowd bombarded the Guardians with questions, many of them searching and most of them hostile. The *Bradford Observer*, which was a local newspaper,

reported in full what was said at the meeting. These extracts from that report show that the townspeople were suspicious of rules made in London, and were afraid that their Board of Guardians would be dominated by the London-based Poor Law Commission. Furthermore, they were afraid that the Commissioners were going to ignore the special problems arising from the sort of periodic unemployment which was found in industrial towns like Bradford, and would force all paupers to go inside a workhouse.

One of the Guardians, a wealthy mill-owner called Mr Lister, agreed to answer any questions and explain any parts of the new Poor Law which the people did not understand:

'Mr Lister: You might as well try to stop up the Ganges [*a river in India*] as to prevent this bill being carried into effect. (Loud cries of disapprobation, which lasted some time.) It is the law of the land, and as such it ought to be obeyed, and will be enforced ultimately, either in its present form or with some amendment. Whatever is the law of the country we must abide by it; if you think it wants alteration, you can seek it through petitions and remonstrances to your representatives in Parliament; but you should not violently oppose it.

Operative: Are the Guardians the servants of the rate-payers or of the Commissioners?

Mr Lister: Of the rate-payers.

Operative: Then the rate-payers say the poor shall be relieved as they have been hitherto, and that they do not want the New Act!

Mr Lister: The Guardians have to go by the Act of Parliament.

Operative: The people of Huddersfield have prevented the introduction of the Poor Law into their town . . . Why cannot the people of Bradford do the same?

Mr Power, the Assistant Commissioner, tried to explain that it *was* possible for the rules to be varied, and that no rule had been made for Bradford which would send all paupers into the workhouse:

'Mr Power: I am aware that in other parts [*of the country*] severer regulations have been issued to the Guardians, restraining them to give relief in the workhouse instead of out of doors. In the regulations given to the Guardians of this Union, there is no such provision, nor is there one rule which restricts the Guardians either as to the amount of relief or the manner of giving it.'

Mr Peter Bussey, one of the leaders of the Bradford anti-Poor Law campaign, asked Mr Power whether the Commissioners were determined to carry the Poor Law into effect in Bradford in opposition to the wishes of the rate-payers. At that, Mr Power refused to discuss the matter further, saying that the Guardians should be allowed to get on with the business of the meeting.

The Chairman, Henry Leah, grew more and more uneasy as the meeting went on. Time and time again he told the crowd that he would resign if 'any harsh or inhuman regulations are proposed'. The meeting was finally adjourned until 10th November, and the Guardians left the Court House. The Assistant Commissioner, Mr Power, had a rough passage on his way out. He was pelted with stones and mud, and hit in the face by a tin can as he ran for the safety of the Sun Inn where he was staying.

Soldiers and Stones

Worse was to come. The meeting due to be held on 10th November was put back by the Guardians until 13th November for fear of what the crowd might do. It was not held on 13th November either, but was postponed for a further week. Mr Power, the Assistant Commissioner, grew alarmed. He was afraid of what these delays might do to the temper of the townspeople. He therefore arranged for soldiers to be sent to Bradford in case of trouble.

When the Guardians met at 10 o'clock on 20th November, there were no more than about 100 people around the Court House. By mid-day, however, the crowd had swelled to 5–6,000, and they began to throw stones at the Court House windows. At this point, one of the magistrates sent for the soldiers. It was then that the rioting began in earnest. The crowd pelted the soldiers with stones, and some had their heads cut open. The soldiers charged the crowd and hit out with the flat of their swords.

These disturbances went on throughout the meeting. When the frightened Guardians left, they were followed by hundreds of people, hooting and jeering and throwing stones. The crowds would not break up and go home, and so the magistrates sent to Leeds for more soldiers. By 10 o'clock that night the streets were clear, but the soldiers were kept on duty until 5 o'clock in the morning.

The situation was clearly very difficult. The new Poor Law was not going to be introduced into Bradford without a struggle. The Guardians were desperately worried. They had been planning and working for the introduction of the new rules for months. Now it seemed that violent opposition could bring all their plans to nothing. They could give in to the demands of the protesters and refuse to bring in the new Poor Law, but this would mean facing the wrath of the Poor Law Commissioners in London, and possibly of the government itself. Or they could bring in the new Poor Law and face rioting and opposition from the very people the Law was supposed to help. They decided to go ahead with what they thought was right. In the spring of 1838 everything which the Guardians had planned and argued for was introduced into Bradford. The new Poor Law was in force.

As the Poor Law Commissioners introduced the new Poor Law throughout the towns and cities of the north, they trod very warily. There was often violent opposition to their plans. The place which put up the longest fight was the town of Todmorden, about twenty miles from Manchester. The opposition there was led by the local MP and mill-owner, John Fielden. Indeed, it was not until long after his death that, in 1877, a workhouse was finally built in the Todmorden Union. However, by 1840 most opposition was at an end, and 95 per cent of all the parishes in England were applying the new Poor Law.

Poverty and Politics

The Poor Law Commission, which was based in London and which had been responsible for bringing the new Poor Law into operation, was very influential. It controlled and organised an enormous undertaking – the relief of poverty. Many people began to believe that such an organisation should be more under the direct control of the government. The Commissioners themselves began to be criticised.

In 1842 Parliament allowed the Commission to continue for another five years, but reduced the number of Assistant Commissioners from twelve to nine. The scandal of the Andover workhouse, where starving paupers were discovered sucking the marrow from bones, showed the whole country that the Commission was not working as it should. It gave the enemies of the Commission an opportunity to press for it to be abolished. In 1847 the Home Secretary disbanded the Commission, and set up instead a Poor Law Board. The President of this Board had to be a Member of Parliament with a place in the government.

The government thus became directly involved with the relief of poverty. However, all the old attitudes were still there behind the new Poor Law. Poverty, most people believed, was the fault of the poor. People became paupers because they were too idle to find work. It was this attitude which prevented other causes of poverty being investigated.

Think carefully about what you have just read, and then answer this question:

There was serious opposition to the introduction of the new Poor Law in the north of England, and some opposition to its introduction in the south. Why, then, did the government insist that the new Poor Law should be enforced throughout the country?

4

SOCIAL REFORM

Town Life for the Labouring Poor

Frederick Engels, the son of a wealthy German cotton manufacturer, visited England in 1842 and worked in Manchester for two years. His shock at what he saw led him to write a book called *The Condition of the Working Class in England*, which was published in 1844. In his book Engels described the conditions in some of Manchester's worst housing:

'. . . There is no artificial floor; kitchen, living and sleeping room all in one. In such a hole, barely six feet long by six broad, I found two beds – such bedsteads and beds! – which, with a staircase and chimney place, exactly filled the room . . . Everywhere before the doors refuse and offal; that any sort of pavement lay underneath could not be seen but only felt, here and there, with the feet . . .'

There were many descriptions from British and foreign writers which told the same story. How had this happened? How had it come about that, in fast-growing, prosperous industrial towns like Leeds, Manchester and Bradford, people lived like this?

Houses

It was because the towns were growing so fast that living conditions for the poor were so bad. The factories, mines and mills were expanding, and needed more and more men and women to work in them. People moved into the towns in order to work as factory hands, and also as cabinet makers, hatters, joiners, engineers, crossing-sweepers and washerwomen. These people had to live somewhere. Tens of thousands of new houses were built quickly and cheaply. Builders and landlords were anxious to make a quick profit. They were not concerned about the comfort and well-being of the people who were to live in them. Many employers neither knew nor cared how their workers lived. They needed a work-force, and maximum profits. And so the houses were built – in long terraces, in square courtyards and in tall tenements. In many towns they were built 'back-to-back' to save space (look at Source A, page 63); bricks, timber, tiles and slates used were the cheapest possible, walls were thin and floors were usually wooden planks or stone slabs put down over the earth.

The type of house a working-class family lived in depended very much, of course, on the family income. It also depended upon the cost of housing in the city in which a family lived. Skilled artisans could usually afford to live in a four-roomed house (a 'two-up, two-down'). Many unskilled workers rented a 'one-up, one-down' house, whilst the poorest families could not afford to rent a whole house of any size, and lived in cellars and single rooms. A lot of working-class families took in a lodger or two. These were usually young, single people who had moved into the town to work. It was an arrangement which suited everyone concerned. The families had a little extra income, and the lodgers somewhere to live in an overcrowded city.

Not all the houses in which the poor lived were new in the nineteenth century. Many of the big cities – particularly London – had large, old houses. These were bought by landlords looking for a quick profit, and divided into hundreds of tiny living spaces for poor families to rent. The destitute lived rough under bridges, in derelict buildings and on rooftops.

Drains, Sewers and Cesspits

Thousands and thousands of houses and tenements in the towns and cities of Britain, where labouring people lived, were not connected to drains or sewers of any kind. The people who lived in them usually had to share a privy with many other families. There was no running water – nothing to flush the waste away. Sometimes it was covered with earth, and sometimes with cold ashes from people's fires. The stench was tremendous. In 1845 houses in Leeds were described as being:

'. . . wholly unprovided with any form of drainage or arrangements for cleansing, one mass of damp and filth. The ashes, garbage and filth of all kinds are thrown from the doors and windows of the houses upon the surface of the streets. The privies are few in proportion to the number of inhabitants. They are open to view both in front and rear and are invariably in a filthy condition and often remain without the removal of any portion of the filth for 6 months . . .'
(From *Parliamentary Papers*, 1845, vol 3)

Lavatories were usually outside, in the courtyards and alleys, and emptied into cesspits. Human waste collected in these cesspits, which were, from time to time, cleaned out by 'night-soil' men. They piled what they had collected in huge dunghills and then sold it off to local farmers. A doctor in Greenock, Scotland, reported that:

'In one part of Market Street is a dunghill, yet it is too large to be called a dunghill. I do not mistake

Sketches of Birmingham slums

its size when I say it contains 100 cubic yards of impure filth collected from all parts of the town. It is never removed; it is the stock in trade of a person who deals in dung . . .'

(From *Parliamentary Papers*, 1842, vol 20)

Some middle-class houses had inside lavatories which flushed. When they flushed, the contents went into one of two places. The house might have a cesspit in the basement, or it might be connected to a sewer. The sewer, however, was only a collecting point. Both cesspits and sewers had to be emptied every so often by the night-soil men. Sometimes, in areas where there were not enough night-soil men, human waste was dumped straight into the nearest river, or left in heaps to seep through the ground into wells and springs.

Water

Water was needed by rich and poor alike for drinking, washing and cooking. The wealthy and the middle classes had water running in pipes to their homes. This water would be sold to them by a water company. However, because the water did not flow all the time, their houses usually had large storage tanks in which to store enough water to make sure that they and their families could have water whenever they wanted to use it.

In the poorer areas of towns and cities, water was not piped to the houses. There were stand-pipes in the streets at which poor people queued with buckets, kettles and saucepans in order to buy water whenever the supply was turned on. Water companies charged for this service. Where there were too few stand-pipes, or none at all, people had to take their water from polluted rivers, streams and wells. The very poor used as little water as possible (because of the cost) and kept it standing for a long time in dirty buckets and pans.

Dirt and Disease

It had been known for hundreds of years that there was some sort of connection between dirt and disease. Dirty living conditions meant that disease flourished. Crowded living conditions meant that disease spread quickly. What was not known, however, was the reason why diseases and infections seemed to flourish in dirty conditions. This was not understood until the

This cartoon was published in the satirical magazine Punch *in 1852. Why do you think it was called 'A Court for King Cholera'?*

1860s, when Louis Pasteur discovered that germs caused disease, and that it was not disease which caused germs.

People found it hard to keep themselves clean. Men, women and children often had body lice which tended to spread typhus fever, from which many died. There were epidemics of typhus in 1837 and 1839; in 1847 'Irish fever' (typhus) killed nearly 10,000 people in north-west England alone. Influenza, scarlet fever, tuberculosis and measles were often killers. Typhoid and diarrhoea were common. Between 1837 and 1840 smallpox raged throughout the country, killing over 10,000 people and scarring many more for life.

However, the disease which was feared above all the others was cholera.

Cholera hit Britain in four massive epidemics: 1831–2, 1848–9, 1853–4 and 1866. The first epidemic left 31,000 dead; the second 62,000.

This is how cholera symptoms were described in 1832:

> 'Vomiting or purging come on; the features become sharp and contracted, the eye sinks; the lips, face, neck, hands and feet and soon after the thighs, arms and whole surface assume a leaden, blue, purple, black or deep brown tint; the pulse becomes small as a thread or else totally extinct. The skin is deadly cold, the tongue flabby and chilled like a piece of dead flesh. The patient speaks in a whisper. He struggles for breath. Sometimes there are rigid spasms of the legs, thighs and loins.'

Cholera was terrifying because it was both swift and deadly. It could kill a healthy person within thirty-six hours – and no one knew how or why.

Local Government

Improvement Acts

Many town corporations and groups of influential people asked Parliament to pass private Acts of Parliament which allowed them to force the introduction of such things as lighting and sewerage into their towns. However, because these Acts were private, they only applied to the town, or group of towns, which asked for them. Between 1831 and 1832, for example, the county of Lancashire had an Act passed for 'Lighting with gas the Town of Saint Helens'; the City of Exeter asked for an 'Act for Better paving, lighting, watching, cleansing and otherwise improving the City of Exeter'. These, and many other, private Acts of Parliament allowed Improvement Commissioners to be elected by rate-payers to deal with the specific problems detailed by the Act. Many towns ended up with different sets of Improvement Commissioners dealing with separate town improvements.

Corruption and Collapse

By the 1830s many people were beginning to use the word 'corrupt' to describe the corporations and Improvement Commissions. By this they meant that elections for the posts of mayor and aldermen were rarely held; corporations passed local laws which were only for the benefit of small groups of citizens; and although many corporations were supposed to administer charities for the benefit of certain citizens, too often the money was used for the private enjoyment of the mayor and corporation.

The Industrial Revolution brought further problems. Towns grew rapidly:

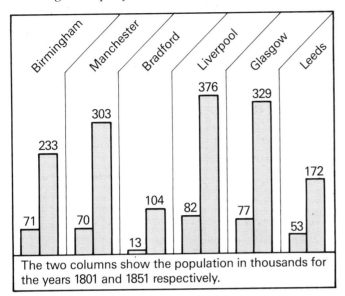

The two columns show the population in thousands for the years 1801 and 1851 respectively.

By the 1830s, however, none of the different systems of local government could cope with the problems of housing, sanitation and disease which came with the rapid growth of industrial towns.

The Municipal Corporations Act, 1835

The first House of Commons elected under the 1832 Reform Act was determined to change the way that town governments were elected, just as the parliamentary electoral system had been changed. In July 1833 the government set up a Royal Commission. This consisted of twenty Commissioners who were mainly lawyers.

The Commissioners acted quickly. They visited 285 towns and investigated the workings of 246 corporations. In March 1835 they presented their findings to the Home Secretary. Although they did not suggest how the situation could be changed, the Commissioners made it clear that reform of the borough and town corporations was absolutely necessary.

In June 1835 Lord John Russell introduced the Municipal Corporations Bill into the House of Commons. You read in Chapter 1 how he had introduced the Reform Bill into the Commons. Would this Bill be as controversial? The House of Commons had a majority of Whigs who were determined to see the Bill passed. Tories, however, were dominant in the Lords and were determined to defend the Tory corporations which they saw as their power base in the country.

The Bill proposed that town councils should replace all the existing systems which operated in boroughs and towns with corporations. Members of a town council were to be elected for periods of three years, with one third of the members retiring from the council each year. Every male householder who had lived in the borough for three years or more would be entitled to vote.

MPs made no serious objections to the Bill, and it was passed by the Commons in July 1835. Many members of the House of Lords, however, regarded the corporations as standing for much of what they regarded as important in the old way of government. Lord Lyndhurst warned the House of Lords that if the corporations fell, 'the Church would come next, and then the hereditary peerage'. However, despite this dramatic warning, the Bill was returned to the House of Commons with only minor changes made to it.

The Bill which finally became law, late in 1835, applied to 178 boroughs. These boroughs were to be run by town councils, which consisted of councillors, aldermen and a mayor. The councillors were elected by all the male rate-payers who had lived in the town for three years or more. Councillors were elected for three years only. The councillors voted from among themselves for a mayor and aldermen. Mayors were elected each year, but aldermen could stay in office for six years. One third of all councillors had to retire from the council each year, and one half of the aldermen every three years. All retiring councillors and aldermen were eligible for re-election.

The Municipal Corporations Act created one standard system of government for the old town and borough corporations. If a town had not been a borough before 1835, it could apply to have a new style corporation. Large industrial towns did this. Manchester, for example, applied for incorporation in 1839. The business of incorporation was expensive and sometimes controversial. Gradually, however, more and more people realised the advantages of having an elected system of local government which could introduce improvements in such things as housing, sanitation, paving and roads. However, the Act did not compel town councils to do anything at all about roads, drains and refuse collection: it simply set up the framework within which it was possible for improvements to take place if the rate-payers of a town wanted them to.

Public Health

Surveys and Reports

The cholera epidemic of 1831–2 (see page 59), started off a wave of investigations into the ways in which people lived in the cellars, courts and tenements of the rapidly growing industrial towns. Some of these investigations and reports were made by doctors who had been shocked by what they had seen as they tried to care for the sick and the dying. Others were made by the many statistical societies, and by private groups such as the Bradford Woolcombers Protective Society. One of the aims of all these investigations was to get the government to act.

By the late 1830s the government had set up enquiries of its own, and these, too, produced reports. Among the most important were the *Report of the Select Committee on the Health of Towns*, which was published in 1840; the *Report from the Poor Law Commissioners on an Enquiry into the Sanitary Conditions of the Labouring Population of Great Britain*, which was published in 1842; and two mammoth reports, which were published in 1844 and 1845, from the 'Commission for Inquiring into the State of Large Towns and Populous Districts'.

Evidence was pouring in from all over the country of towns and cities which were simply unable, or unwilling, to cope with the sanitation problems which had been created by the rapid growth of industrial towns. There were reports of sewage heaps of between twenty-five and thirty-five thousand tons piling up in the middle of cities; in Lancashire it was normal for forty people to have to share the same privy; in Liverpool a regulation was discovered which forbade water closets to be connected to sewers.

Burial grounds and cemeteries were reported to be so packed with bodies that bones could be seen sticking up through the earth. In London, Burnhill Fields, which was a 4-acre burial ground, contained 100,000 corpses. Every year 50,000 dead were added to London's 200 acres of cemeteries. Epidemics caused even greater pressure on available land, and not only in London.

The *Report from the Poor Law Commissioners on an Enquiry into the Sanitary Conditions of the Labouring Population of Great Britain* was largely the work of Edwin Chadwick. (You read about him on pages 36–7.) Chadwick arranged for his enquiry to be set up after reading reports which the Poor Law Commission had collected about the ways in which epidemics like cholera had increased the cost of the poor-rate. One of the things which Chadwick showed in this Report was that where a person lived and what job they had were of vital importance in deciding how long they lived:

Average age of death in:	Manchester	Liverpool	Rutland
Professional people, gentry and their families:	38 years	35 years	52 years
Tradesmen, farmers and their families	20 years	22 years	41 years
Labourers and their families	17 years	15 years	38 years

The main cause of disease, Edwin Chadwick decided, was that townspeople breathed in air which had been poisoned by filth. Many people shared his ideas about the way in which disease was spread. Chadwick suggested several ways in which the spread of diseases could be stopped. All of them were linked to the miasmic theory – the belief that bad smells and filth in the air caused illness. The Report recommended that streets should be cleaned and drainage improved; houses had better ventilation (which would let in more air and sunlight); and that sewerage systems and water supplies should be introduced. Edwin Chadwick emphasised the need for a national body to organise huge engineer-

A notice issued by the Dudley Board of Health

ing schemes to improve sewerage and sanitation. Perhaps most importantly of all, this Report showed that bad living conditions could not always be blamed on the poor themselves.

The Public Health Act, 1848

In Britain, before 1848, there was no organised system of public health. In the 1840s the idea grew that what was needed was one single body to be responsible for all aspects of public health, such as water supplies, sewerage, drainage and cleansing. A few of the new councils tried to work through Improvement Acts. In 1846 Liverpool showed what could be done. The city had its own Sanitary Act, which made the council responsible for drainage, paving, sewerage and cleansing, and appointed Dr. W. H. Duncan as their first Medical Officer of Health. However, not all towns and boroughs were as enterprising. Many could not follow the example set by Liverpool because of opposition from the old Improvement Commissions to giving up their powers, and opposition from the water companies who would lose their profits. Most towns and boroughs carried on in the old ways, falling deeper and deeper into administrative muddle.

The Public Health Act was passed by the House of Commons in 1848. It established a central Board of Health with three Commissioners. These Commissioners were Edwin Chadwick, Dr. Southwood Smith (a very able and well respected doctor) and Lord Shaftesbury.

(Lord Shaftesbury was born in 1801 and was called Anthony Ashley Cooper. Because he was the son of a lord, he was given the title Lord Ashley. He was known as Lord Ashley when he entered Parliament in 1826. It was not until 1861 that he inherited the title 'Earl of Shaftesbury'. However, in order to be clear, and because he is usually referred to by his title, he is called Lord Shaftesbury throughout this book.)

This central Board of Health supervised the setting

Sitting of the Board of Health, Gwydyr House, Whitehall in 1849

up of local Boards of Health in towns which did not already have one. Local Boards had the power to see that sewerage systems were built, streets were cleaned, street lighting was introduced and houses were built to certain regulations regarding space, light and drainage. Local Boards could appoint Officers of Health, and were allowed to collect rates so that sewers could be covered, cleansed and emptied, and houses connected to sewers and supplied with water.

This Act, however, did not apply to all towns. It applied to towns and cities only if one tenth of all rate-payers wanted it to. The only places which had to come under the Act were those where the death rate was higher than the national average (more than twenty-three deaths in any one year for every thousand people living in the town). The Act made it possible for all Edwin Chadwick's recommendations to be brought into effect – but only if conditions in a town were desperate, or if influential people wanted them to be brought in.

Gains and Losses

By 1854, 182 local Boards of Health had been set up, and only thirteen of them had completed sewerage and water-work schemes. Only thirty Medical Officers of Health had been appointed. However, those towns which did have local Boards of Health usually showed a marked improvement in the overall health of the people who lived there.

Towns like Macclesfield, for example, reduced their death rate from forty-two per thousand in 1847 to twenty-six per thousand in 1858. In the north-east, Dr. S.E. Piper, who was the Medical Officer of Health for Darlington, reported that:

> 'Water had been introduced into our streets . . .
> new sewers and drains were in effective operation
> . . . cesspools abolished . . . when epidemic diseases
> again appeared they could not maintain a footing
> in the old haunts where they formerly lingered . . .'

Other local Boards, like the one in Bridgend, Glamorgan, wound down their activities once the cholera threat of 1838–9 had passed:

> ' . . . the Cholera having ceased for some days in
> this District, the Board consider they may dispense
> with the services of Dr. Camps . . .'

The Board of Health in London faced strong opposition from those who were against what they saw as government interferance. Furthermore, once the cholera epidemic died down, many rate-payers began to complain about the cost of paying for public health improvements. Some of these rate-payers were able to influence their local MPs, and in 1854 the Board of Health was placed under close parliamentary scrutiny, and its very existence had to be renewed each year.

A great deal was still left to local initiative. Towns which had not been incorporated could opt to come under the Municipal Corporations Act; town corporations and councils could decide if the Public Health Act should apply to them. What was important, however, was that the framework for change was there, and could be used by those who wanted it.

SOURCE WORK:
Living Conditions for the Poor

SOURCE A

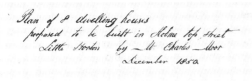

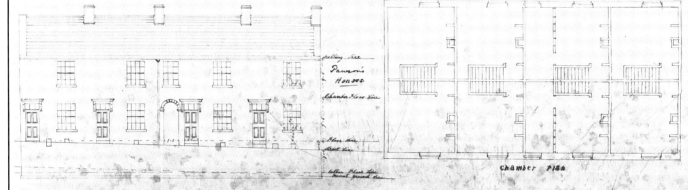

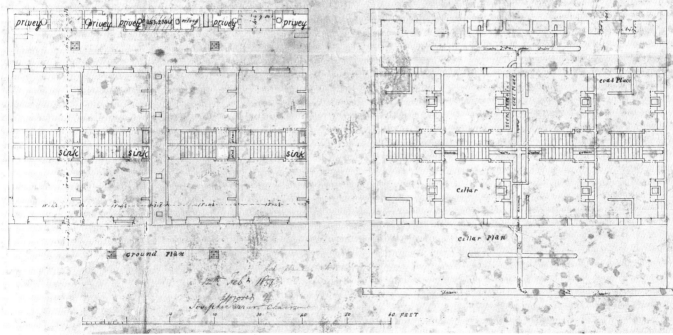

1. Look at Source A carefully. What arrangements did the builders provide for:
   (i) washing?
   (ii) cooking?
   (iii) going to the lavatory?

2. Use Source A and the information in this chapter to describe what everyday life would have been like for the people living in these houses.

Living Conditions for the Poor

SOURCE B

The Bradford Woolcombers Protective Society appointed a 'Sanatory Committee' in May 1845 to find out about the conditions in which the poorest woolcombers lived. This is part of their report on the Little Horton area:

'Mary Gate 39 – This miserable abode is situated over a privy – the stench is intolerable – only one apartment in which the inmates work and sleep.

Nelson Court – A great many woolcombers reside in this court. It is a perfect nuisance. There are a number of cellars in it utterly unfit for human dwellings. No drainage whatever. The visitors [those people who put the report together] cannot find words to express their horror of the filth, stench, and misery which abounds in this locality, and were unable to bear the overpowering effluvia which emanates from a common sewer which runs from the Unitarian Chapel beneath the houses. Were this to be fully described the Committee might subject themselves to the charge of exaggeration. We trust that some of those in affluent circumstances, will visit these abodes of misery and disease.'

2. Now read Source B, which is describing part of Little Horton.
   (a) Using your knowledge of the time, explain why the authors of this Report hoped that 'those in affluent circumstances' would visit Nelson Court.
   (b) Would the houses built in Holme Top Street, Little Horton, (Source A) have become, eventually, like the houses described in Source B?

SOURCE C

This letter was published in The Times newspaper on 5th July 1849. It had fifty-four signatures.

'Sur,

May we beg and beseech your proteckshion and power. We are Sur, as it may be, livin in a wilderness so far as the rest of london knows anything of us, or as the rich and great people care about. We live in muck and filthe. We aint got no privez, no dust bins, no water supplies, no drain or suer in the whole place. The Suer Company in Greek Street, Soho Square, all great and powerful men, take no notice wat somedever of our complaints. The stenche of a Gully hole is disgustin. We al of us suffer and numbers are ill and if the Cholera comes lord help us.'

3. (a) Why was this letter written?
   (b) The letter was badly spelt and clearly not written by the sort of people who would read The Times newspaper. What reasons might the editor have had for publishing it?

SOURCE D

This is a description of part of Manchester. It was written by John Roberton, who was a surgeon, and was published in 1840 in the Report of the Committee on the Health of Towns No. xi.

'. . . New cottages, huddled together row behind row, may be seen springing up in many parts, but especially in the township of Manchester, where the land is higher in price than the land for cottage sites in other townships . . . The authorities cannot interfere. A cottage may be badly drained, the streets may be full of pits, brimful of stagnant water, the receptacle of dead cats and dogs, yet no-one may find fault . . . Food is dear, labour scarce, and wages in many branches very low; . . . disease and death are making unusual havoc . . .'

4. Read Source D carefully, and then look back at Sources B and C.
   (a) What similarities can you find between the houses in which the poor lived in Bradford and in London?
   (b) Using the evidence of the sources themselves, explain how likely it was that something would be done to change the conditions in which these people lived.
   (c) How would the 1848 Public Health Act improve the situation?

Living Conditions for the Poor

SOURCE E

The first official census was taken in 1801, but it was little more than just a count of the people living in England and Wales. Later censuses, as you will see from this source, collected a great deal more information.

18   **328**

Name of Street, Place, or Road, and Name or No. of House	Name and Surname of each Person who abode in the house, on the Night of the 30th March, 1851	Relation to Head of Family	Condition	Age of Males	Age of Females	Rank, Profession, or Occupation	Where Born	Whether Blind, or Deaf-and-Dumb
Adelaide Street	John Emmett	Head	Mar	44		Woolcomber	Morton Banks Yorks	
	Hannah Do	Wife	Do				Dewsbury Do	
	Sarah Speding	Step Daur	U	26		Spinner	Kirkstall Do	
	Chas Emmett	Son	Do	11		Do	Do Do	
	Isaac Kood	Man	Do	60		Woolcomber	Bingley Do	
Adelaide Street	Sarah Pickles	Head	W		44		Darlington Durham	
	Mary Ann Do	Daur	U		16	Stuff Weaver	Keighley Do	
	Elizabeth Do	Do	Do		14	Spinner	Do Do	
	John Do	Son	Do	16		Do	Do Do	
Adelaide Street	Richd Smith	Head	Mar	40		Woolcomber	Ireland	
	Mary Do	Wife	Do		34		Do	
	Elizabeth Do	Daur	U	16		Factory Worker	Bradford Yorks	
	John Do	Son	Do	11		Scholar	Do	
	Mary Do	Daur	Do		7	At home	Do	
	Richard Do	Son	Do	4		Do	Do	
	Rosina Do	Daur	Do		2		Do	
	Wm Do	Cousin	Do	29		Woolcomber	Kidderminster	
	Geo Do	Do	Do	17		Do	Do	
	Wm Glesson	Visitor	Do	27		Do	Ireland	
U — B —			Total of Persons...	10	9			D — Eng.

(Page from Census Enumerator's Returns, Little Horton, 1851)

5. This page gives details of three families. They are, however, typical of the families living in the Little Horton area.
   (a) For each family, work out:
      (i) the names of the mother and father;
      (ii) the names and ages of the children;
      (iii) the occupations of the adults and children.

(b) Two families take in lodgers. So did many other families in the area.
   (i) Why would a family of seven, like the Smiths, take in lodgers?
   (ii) Why would people looking for lodgings want to stay in an area like this?

'. . . Exhausted equally in body and mind . . .'

Peter Gaskell, who was a doctor in northern England, wrote a book called *The Manufacturing Population of England*, which was published in 1833. This is part of what he wrote:

'Rising at or before day-break, between four and five o'clock . . . he swallows a hasty meal, or hurries to the mill without taking any food whatever . . . At twelve o'clock, the engine stops, and an hour is given for dinner . . . Again they are closely immured [*kept inside*] from one o'clock till eight or nine, with the exception of twenty minutes, this being allowed for tea . . . when finally dismissed for the day, they are exhausted equally in body and mind . . .'

Working in the Textile Factories and Mills

Before textile factories and mills were built, men, women and children spun thread and wove cloth in their own homes. The development of machines worked by water-power meant that factories and mills could be built, and for the first time workers were crowded together in one building to produce cloth. The first factory of this kind was built in 1717. The develop-ment of coal-fired boilers which produced steam to drive machinery took a long time. It was not until the 1830s that their use became widespread. Mills and factories did not have to be built in river valleys any more. They could be built anywhere, as long as there were sufficient people living close enough to provide a work-force, and as long as coal could be brought to the factory site. Factories were planned so that the new machinery would work smoothly and efficiently. Little or no thought was given to the people who had to work these machines.

Cotton, for example, had to be spun at a certain temperature, and the workers simply had to cope. William Cobbett, writing in the *Political Register* in 1824, described working conditions in a cotton mill:

'In the cotton spinning work, these creatures are kept . . . in a heat of from 80 to 84 degrees . . . The door of the place wherein they work, is locked, except half an hour at tea time, the people are not allowed to send for water to drink, in the hot factory . . . In addition, there are the dust, and what is called cotton-flyings or fuz, which the unfortunate creatures have to inhale; and the fact is, . . . that well constituted men are rendered old and past labour at forty years of age, and the children rendered decrepit and deformed . . .'

Accidents and illness were common. You read in the last section (page 61) about the *Report on the Sanitary Conditions of the Labouring Population*. In this Report, the Poor Law Commissioners described how unfenced

This picture, 'Carding, Drawing and Roving in a Cotton Mill', was first printed in a book by Edward Baines called History of the Cotton Manufacture in Great Britain *which was published in 1835. The mill may look light and airy inside, but in reality it would have been hot, humid and noisy, full of the smell of engine oil and working machinery, and with air that was thick with cotton fluff*

machinery in factories meant that hair and clothing were often caught in the various moving parts:

'. . . many are caused by loose portions of dress being caught by the machinery, so as to drag the unfortunate sufferers under its power. The shawls of females, or their long hair, and the aprons and loose sleeves of the boys and men, are in this way frequent causes of dreadful mutilation . . .'

The damp conditions in which the cotton had to be spun led to all kinds of diseases connected with breathing, such as bronchitis, and an illness called 'factory fever' which was a kind of typhus. The long hours men, women and children spent bent over machinery, or doing the same repetitive job, led to their bodies developing deformities.

Mill-owners sometimes employed whole families, and all members of the family, even the children, had to work long hours to earn enough to be able to survive. Small children were particularly useful because they could crawl underneath machinery, whilst it was still working, to clear away waste cotton and fluff. Their small fingers were particularly useful, too, in piecing together broken threads.

The larger textile factories employed overseers. They were paid according to the amount of work produced by the men, women and children who worked under them. Therefore working hours were usually long, and overseers (and some parents) often took advantage of the children who worked with them. It was common, in the 1820s, for children aged seven years old to work from 6 am to 7 pm with only an hour off for meals. Rules in factories were strict. For example, workers were fined for lateness and for talking to each other.

Sometimes they were paid, not with money, but in tokens. These tokens could only be exchanged for goods at a 'tommy shop'. These 'tommy shops' were owned by the employers who could, of course, charge whatever prices they liked.

However, not all manufacturers ran their mills and factories in the same way. In Scotland, a man called Robert Owen became general manager and part owner of David Dale's New Lanark Mills in 1799. He tried out a new system. Robert Owen believed that people would work best when their living and working conditions were good. Working-hours in his mills were therefore reduced to ten and a half per day, and no child under the age of ten was allowed to work. Workers were paid when they were sick, and wages generally were higher than in other mills and factories. Good housing, with sanitation, was provided for the workers, and schools for their children. A general store sold basic goods at cost price. Many employers who were used to the traditional system mocked Robert Owen. But his work-force seemed healthy and contented, and his mills ran at a profit.

Why did the government not step in and insist on decent, safe and healthy working conditions in factories and mills? Up until the nineteenth century, governments were mainly concerned only with defence, for which they collected taxes, and with the overall maintaining of order in the country. The government was simply not expected to interfere in the way in which people ran their everyday lives. Therefore it was not surprising that the government, and many other people, believed that it was none of their business to interfere in how a factory or mill owner treated the men, women and children he employed.

This contemporary drawing shows a school room in Robert Owen's mills at New Lanark

Factory Reform

Yorkshire Slavery

On 16th October 1830 a letter was printed in a local Leeds newspaper, the *Leeds Mercury*, under the heading 'Yorkshire Slavery'. This is part of what it said:

> 'Let the truth speak out . . . Thousands of our fellow-creatures and fellow-subjects, both male and female, the inhabitants of a Yorkshire town . . . are at this very moment existing in a state of slavery more horrid than are the victims of that hellish system – colonial slavery . . . [*they*] are compelled, not by the cart-whip of the negro slave-driver, but by the dread of the equally appalling thong or strap of the overlooker, to hasten half dressed . . . to those magazines of British Infantile Slavery – the Worsted Mills in the town and neighbourhood of Bradford! . . . Thousands of little children . . . are daily compelled to labour, from six o'clock in the morning to seven in the evening with only – Britons, blush whilst you read it! – with only thirty minutes allowed for eating and recreation . . . .'

Parliament was, at this time, considering outlawing slavery in the British colonies. One of the strongest opponents of slavery was William Wilberforce, who was one of Yorkshire's MPs. Now here was someone saying that something very like slavery existed in Yorkshire itself – in the worsted mills of Bradford.

This letter was the first of a series. The man who wrote the 'Yorkshire Slavery' letters was Richard Oastler, a forty-one-year-old Yorkshireman. He lived in Fixby Hall, near Huddersfield in the West Riding, and was steward of the Fixby estate there. Richard Oastler was a strong Anglican and a Tory. It was through his friendship with the Tory mill owner John Wood that he first heard about the working conditions in Bradford mills.

Early Reformers

There was a Tory tradition of taking care of the people who made you your wealth. An example of this was Sir Robert Peel. He was the wealthy owner of a number of cotton mills in Lancashire, a local squire and a Tory MP. In the 1780s he employed over a thousand children in his mills. Together with other members of his family he employed most of the working people in Bury, Lancashire. He was shocked by the maltreatment of apprentices in some of the cotton mills which belonged to other owners. Because of this he was behind the Health and Morals of Apprentices Act of 1802, which limited to twelve the number of hours a cotton apprentice could work.

Robert Owen, about whom you read on page 67, began a campaign in 1815 to limit to ten and a half the number of hours any child could work. Investigations, by a Committee of the House of Commons and by two House of Lords Committees, followed. In 1815 an Act sponsored by Sir Robert Peel limited to twelve hours the

Children at work in the 1820s winding cotton in a mill

time any child could work in a cotton mill.

About this time, many cotton mill workers – the operatives – began to think that something ought to be done about the long hours which they worked. In 1814 the Manchester Operatives Committee was formed. Anglican priests and doctors collected evidence and published information about local working hours and conditions. Nothing, however, was organised on a larger scale.

Bradford, on the eastern side of the Pennines, was a town where the mills specialised in making worsted, which was a particular sort of woollen cloth. In 1825 three wealthy Tory mill owners, John Wood, John Rand and Matthew Thompson, tried to persuade their fellow mill owners to agree to reduce the hours worked in their mills. They believed that no one should work for longer than ten hours. They failed. Not only did the other mill owners fear that their profits would fall, but they believed that their operatives had a right to work for as long a day as they wanted.

The Ten-Hours Movement

Richard Oastler's 'Yorkshire Slavery' letters were, therefore, part of a general movement among some workers and some mill owners to reduce working hours. Oastler wrote the letters, too, because he believed that a highly charged emotional appeal would be the best way to reach people's consciences. Pressure for change, he thought, would follow, and it would not be long before the right sort of legislation would be passed by Parliament.

However, events did not quite turn out like that. Richard Oastler's letters sparked off a furious controversy in the Yorkshire Press. Edward Baines, the editor of the *Leeds Mercury* which had printed the 'Yorkshire Slavery' letters, supported parliamentary reform (see page 22) and the rights of the industrial towns to be represented in Parliament. His newspaper eventually came out in strong support of owners like John Marshall of Leeds, Jonathan Akroyd of Halifax and William Ackroyd of Otley, and of their right to employ their workers freely and without the interference of Parliament. On the other hand, newspapers like the *Intelligencer* and the *Patriot*, which were bought, read and owned by old-fashioned Tories, were in favour of legislation. They were supported by men like John Wood, by some of the operatives themselves, and by Richard Oastler.

The controversy raged throughout the winter of 1830–1, with letters and articles in all the papers involved, doing their best to pour scorn on the opinions and attitudes of the other side.

A new Factory Act was passed by Parliament in 1831. It applied to cotton factories only. No child under the age of nine was allowed to work in them, all sorts of proposals had been accepted which limited the length of 'night', and which, therefore, extended the time period during which children over the age of nine were available for work, which was during the 'day'. Perhaps most significantly of all, there was no way in which employers could be made to obey the Act.

Richard Oastler was furious. A Bill which would have made a great difference to the lives of working children had been virtually wrecked by the interests of the manufacturers. Oastler knew that groups of workers in Huddersfield, Leeds, Bradford and Keighley had formed 'Short-Time Committees' to press for a shorter working day for everyone who worked in factories and mills. In June 1831 he agreed to join forces with them to fight for a ten-hour working day for all. By the autumn, Oastler was urging operatives to set up committees in every manufacturing town and village, to collect information and to publish facts.

This was a new sort of organisation. Operating from taverns, the committee network spread throughout the textile districts of England and Scotland. The committees were usually financed by Tory industrialists who thought of themselves as father-figures in their mills and factories, by Anglican clergy and by Tory squires. The actual workers on the committees were usually those factory and mill operatives who wanted change (and not all did), tradesmen and shopkeepers. And so an organised campaign began for a Ten-Hours Bill.

Fixby Hall, Richard Oastler's home, became the planning centre of the Ten-Hours Movement. Richard Oastler was the central organiser, who co-ordinated the work of all the committees and controlled the central funds which were mainly his own private savings and John Wood's sizeable contributions. A great winter campaign of rallies, speeches and processions was organised, and it was Richard Oastler who injected fire into the Movement. He wrote in 1832:

'Operatives, – This Cause is your own. Never desert it. Bend your thoughts always to it – publish the Horrors of the System – subscribe what you can, by what you can – and be assured God will prosper the right. Oppression has reigned long enough. Let the Nation see you have resolved your Sons and Daughters shall be free . . . Be united. Be firm. Be courteous and obedient to your Masters – but resolutely bent on using every means the Law provides, to remove slavery from your helpless little ones. God bless you and the Holy cause.'

Michael Sadler, the House of Commons and the Select Committee

Meetings and rallies, pamphlets and speeches could not make laws. If any lasting change was to be made to people's working hours in factories and mills, an MP had to be found who would rally support in Parliament and introduce a Ten-Hours Bill.

Michael Sadler was an MP who supported the aims of the Ten-Hours Movement. He was a close friend of Richard Oastler. A Tory and an Anglican, Sadler had been born in Leeds, and had spent some years working in his family's linen business before entering Parliament.

In March 1832 Michael Sadler introduced a Bill into the Commons which proposed that no child who was under the age of nine years old should enter a factory;

Richard Oastler

young people aged between nine and eighteen should work no more than a ten-hour day, and there should be no night work at all for anyone aged under twenty-one.

This was just what the Ten-Hours Movement wanted. Quickly their organisation swang into action. A campaign of rallies and speeches, backed up with pamphlets, broadsides and letters to newspapers swept the country.

A Select Committee of the House of Commons, with Sadler as Chairman, was set up to enquire into the facts of the case for a shorter working week.

Richard Oastler and everyone in the Ten-Hours Movement put an enormous amount of energy into preparing evidence for the Select Committee. They insisted that men, women and children should give evidence only about their own experiences. Half-remembered horror stories told to them by other people would not do. The leaders of the Movement chose with great care the witnesses who would appear before Sadler's Committee. Of course, only those whose evidence would put the best case for a Ten-Hours Bill were selected. The report of the Select Committee was published in January 1833. It provided shocking revelations about factory hours and conditions, and brought the whole issue to the attention of people who had been totally unaware of what was happening.

A month before the publication of the Report, Parliament had been dissolved. Elections were to be held as a result of the Reform Act of 1832, about which you read on page 25. The borough of Leeds was to be rep-resented in Parliament for the first time. Michael Sadler stood for election as their MP, and was defeated. Richard Oastler was convinced that the Reform Act itself had damaged the Ten-Hours Movement. The Act had, he argued, given more power and influence to the manufacturers. It was these very manufacturers who tended to oppose factory reform and the Ten-Hours Movement. The defeat of Michael Sadler was a great blow to the Movement. A new Parlaimentary spokes-man had to be found, and somehow the Movement had to keep up pressure at Westminster in support of the findings of Michael Sadler's Select Committee, which had just been published.

Lord Shaftesbury, the Royal Commission and Parliament

In January 1833 twenty delegates from Short-Time Committees in Scotland, Nottingham, Lancashire and Yorkshire met in Bradford to consider the situation. They agreed that the Rev. George Stringer Bull should choose a new parliamentary leader. He approached the Tory evangelical Lord Shaftesbury, who agreed to give the Ten-Hours Movement his support. Shaftesbury was as good as his word. On 5th March 1833, only a month into the new parliamentary session, he introduced a Ten-Hours Bill into the House of Commons.

Many MPs, however, had not been satisfied with the Report from Michael Sadler's Select Committee. They pointed out that it was biased as it only gave the operatives' point of view. The Commons therefore decided to set up a Royal Commission to investigate the working conditions of children in factories.

The Commission worked quickly. Two months later their Report was published. It contained evidence of long working hours and harsh conditions which damaged children and young people. The members of the Commission, two of whom were Edwin Chadwick and Dr. Southwood Smith, who you read about in connection with their work on the Poor Law, were convinced:

'. . that a case was made out for the interference of the Legislature on behalf of the children employed in factories . . '

Parliament, in their judgement, would be quite justified in passing laws to regulate conditions inside mills and factories as they affected children. The Commission criticised the Ten-Hours Movement for trying to introduce a ten-hour working day for all adults by emphasising too strongly the plight of the children. Shaftesbury's Bill was criticised for trying to introduce a ten-hour day for adults, when adults were free agents and should be able to work for as long as they chose. Furthermore, the Commission argued, Shaftesbury's Bill made no provision for the education of children once they finished work.

Reluctantly, Shaftesbury gave up his Bill. On 9th August 1833 a new Bill, prepared by Edwin Chadwick, was introduced to the House of Commons by Althorp. Twenty days later it received the Royal assent.

The 1833 Factory Act

This Act applied to all textile mills and factories, although some of its clauses did not apply to silk or lace mills. It laid down that, with the exception of lace and silk mills, no child under the age of nine could work at all. Children aged nine to thirteen years could work for up to nine hours a day, provided they did not work more than forty-eight hours in any one week. The Act stated that young people aged between fourteen and eighteen could work for up to twelve hours a day, provided they did not work for more than sixty-nine hours a week. No one under the age of eighteen could work at night: their hours had to be put in between 5.30 am and 8.30 pm.

The Act went further than a simple regulation of hours and ages. It stated that children under thirteen had to attend school for two hours a day. It also appointed four Inspectors to make sure that the Act was obeyed.

How Successful was the 1833 Act?

Earlier Factory Acts (1802, 1819 and 1831) had tried to regulate working conditions for children. They had not really worked because Justices of the Peace (JPs) were responsible for seeing that the Acts were obeyed, and many JPs were factory owners.

The 1833 Act, however, was different. Inspectors were not factory owners. Each Inspector had several sub-Inspectors working under him, and so could be reasonably thorough in inspecting the factories for which he was responsible. The problem with enforcing the 1833 Act, however, was that many parents and still more employers lied about the ages of the children. It was not until 1837 that it was made compulsory to register births. Before that, it was up to the parents whether or not their children were baptised at the parish church, and so were entered in the register of births, or not.

Schools, too, were a problem. The Act stated that children working forty-eight hours a week or less had to have two hours of schooling a day. This meant that factory schools had to be established, and, as the Inspectors found, many were very unsatisfactory. Children were too often crowded into boiler rooms and engine sheds, and nothing very worthwhile was taught or learned.

Factory Inspectors allowed the mill owners to work a shift system with the children, provided that the Act was obeyed. Children working shifts had to work the right number of hours in total, and could not work during the hours when they were supposed to be at home. This meant that the mills did not have to close down – and men and women worked as many hours as before.

The 1833 Factory Act had, however, established one very important principle. The government could and should intervene in relationships between employers and their workforce.

A Ten-Hour Day for All?

Many of the supporters of the Ten-Hours Movement became involved in other activities such as Chartism and the agitation against the new Poor Law of 1834. The Movement rallied usually only when a new Factory Act was proposed, and then it tried to arouse public opinion in support of a ten-hour day for all workers. It was left to Lord Shaftesbury to keep the cause of a ten-hour day alive in Parliament.

Lord Shaftesbury was defeated by 138 votes in his attempt to get a 'Ten Hours' clause put into a new Factory Act which was proposed by the Home Secretary James Graham in 1844. The enormous step forward made by this Act, when it became law later in the year, was that, for the very first time, women became 'protected persons' and had their hours of work limited to twelve a day. In order to achieve this, factory owners had to be made a concession: the age at which children could be employed was lowered from nine years to eight. However, these children were only allowed to work for six and a half hours a day instead of nine, and had to have three hours compulsory schooling.

It was not until the following year that Parliament agreed to a ten-hour day for women and children. It was, however, impossible for the mill owners to run their factories for ten hours only each day. They got round the Act by working out a shift system for the women and children – and by making the men work a fifteen or sixteen-hour day.

Clearly the men and women who supported the Ten-Hours Movement were not happy with this arrangement. Women and children had got better working conditions – but at the expense of the men, who had to work longer and longer hours. In 1850 something like a compromise was reached. Parliament agreed to pass an Act which increased the amount of time women and children had to work, but reduced that which men worked. A ten-and-a-half-hour day was to be worked in mills and factories by men, women and children.

In 1866 Lord Shaftesbury remembered that he:

'had to break every political connection, to encounter a most formidable array of capitalists, millowners, doctrinaires, and men, who, by natural impulse, hated all "humanity-mongers".'

Yet, by the middle of the nineteenth century, the battles were over. Samuel Kydd, writing in 1857 about the history of the factory movement, said that the movement:

'. . . occupied many years of the lives of some self-sacrificing, strong-minded, persevering, and benevolent men, . . . and left the mark of its existence on the legislation of the country.'

At Richard Oastler's memorial service in 1861, the Rev. George Stringer Bull was able to say that:

'there is now scarcely a manufacturer to be found, who does not thank God for the factory regulation laws, which were forced from an unwilling government by the energy of Oastler and his friends.'

SOURCE WORK:
Factory Reform

In the early 1830s there were many enquiries made into working conditions in factories and mills. Source A is taken from the *Report of the Select Committee of the House of Commons*, which you read about on pages 69–70. Source B is taken from the *Report of the Royal Commission*, which was set up to investigate the employment of children in factories. You read about this on page 70.

SOURCE A

'Elizabeth Bentley, age 23, lives at Leeds, began work at the age of six in Mr Busk's flax-mill . . . Hours 5am till 9pm, when they were 'thronged', otherwise 6am to 7 at night, with 40 minutes for meal at noon.
– Does that keep you constantly on your feet?
– Yes, there are so many frames, and they run so quick.
– Suppose you flagged a little, or were too late, what would they do?
– Strap us.
– Girls as well as boys?
– Yes.
– Have you ever been strapped?
– Yes.
– Severely?
– Yes.
– Were the girls so struck as to leave marks upon their skin?
– Yes, they have had black marks many a time, and their parents dare not come to him about it, they are afraid of losing their work.'

(From 'Committee on Factory Children's Labour' *Parliamentary Papers (Select Committee)*, vol. XV, 1831–2)

SOURCE B

'I have seen them fall asleep, and they have been performing their work with their hands while they were asleep . . .'

(Evidence given by Joseph Badder, a spinner at Mr Bradley's, Leicester, in *Parliamentary Papers (Royal Commission)*, vol. XX, 1833)

1. (a) What did Elizabeth Bentley say happened to her, and to other children, if their work was not satisfactory?
   (b) What did Joseph Badder say about the children working with him?
   (c) Use the sources and your own knowledge to explain why the children's parents and other adult workers did not complain to the employers about the way in which children were treated.

SOURCE C

This source is an extract from a book written by Andrew Ure (1778–1857) when he was 57. He worked for some time as a Professor of Chemistry in a Scottish university before coming to London in 1834 to work as an analytical chemist to the Board of Customs. He wrote several directories about arts, manufactures and geology, as well as *The Philosophy of Manufacture* from which this extract is taken.

'I have visited many factories, entering the spinning rooms, unexpectedly, and often alone, at different times of the day, and I never saw a single instance of corporal chastisement [*punishment*] inflicted on a child, nor indeed did I ever see children in ill-humour. They seemed to be always cheerful and alert, taking pleasure in the light play of their muscles . . .'

(*The Philosophy of Manufacture*, A. Ure, published in 1835)

2. Now read Source C.
   (a) What does Dr. Ure say about the way in which children were treated in factories?
   (b) Read the following statements carefully, and then answer the question which follows.
      (i) Elizabeth Bentley was remembering how she had been treated when she was a child and worked in a flax mill.
      (ii) Joseph Badder was describing how children were treated in the mill at which he worked.
      (iii) Dr. Ure visited many factories investigating the working conditions of children.
      (iv) Elizabeth Bentley and Joseph Badder were giving evidence to a Parliamentary Commission.
      (v) Dr. Ure was writing a book.
Would Elizabeth Bentley, Joseph Badder or Dr. Ure be the most likely to be a reliable source of evidence about working conditions for children?

Factory Reform

SOURCE D

This source is an extract from a book by Robert Owen. You read about him on page 67. In this extract Robert Owen is writing about the cotton-spinning mills in New Lanark, Scotland, of which he was part owner.

'. . . The practice of employing children in the mills, of six, seven and eight years of age, was discontinued, and their parents advised to allow them to acquire health and education until they were ten years old . . . The children were taught reading, writing and arithmetic during five years, that is, from five to ten, in the village school without expense to their parents . . . Their houses were rendered [*made*] more comfortable, their streets were improved, the best provisions were purchased and sold to them at low rates . . fuel and clothes were obtained for them in the same manner . . . Those employed became industrious, temperate, healthy, faithful to their employers and kind to each other . . .'

(Robert Owen, *A New View of Society*, 1831)

3. Read Source D.
   (a) Describe what Robert Owen believed an employer should do for his work-force.
   (b) What did Robert Owen believe would happen as a result of these actions?
   (c) Did Robert Owen have any proof that his theories would work?

SOURCE E

You read (page 71) that James Graham introduced a new Factory Bill into the House of Commons in 1844. Lord Shaftesbury had tried, and failed, to get a 'Ten-Hours' clause inserted into the Bill. This source is part of James Graham's speech against the inclusion of the 'Ten-Hours' clause. He is quoting from the report of a Mr. Horner, who was made a Factory Inspector after the 1833 Factory Act.

'I have made an estimate of the loss a mill would sustain from working eleven hours a day only instead of twelve, and I find it would amount to £850 per annum. If it were reduced to ten hours, it would be about £1,530 per annum. Unless, therefore, the millowner can obtain a proportionately higher price for the commodity, he must reduce wages or abandon his trade.'

(James Graham, Speech in the House of Commons, debate on the Factory Act, 1844)

4. Which of the following does Mr. Horner say would happen to mill-owners if working hours were reduced to ten a day? Explain your choice carefully.

   (a) They would all go out of business.
   (b) They would all suffer enormous losses.
   (c) They would have to pay their workers less for working the same hours.
   (d) They would have to pay their workers more for working fewer hours.
   (e) They would have to lower the selling price of the material they produced in order to pay their workers more.
   (f) They would have to put up the price of the material they were selling, or their workers' wages would be reduced.

SOURCE F

This is an extract from a speech by John Bright MP. He is speaking against the introduction of the 1844 Factory Act. (Look back to page 71.) John Bright was a leading radical. He was the son of a Rochdale mill owner, and came from a Quaker family. He was MP for Durham in 1843, and represented Manchester from 1847–57.

'. . . The people ask for freedom for their industry, for the removal of the shackles on their trade; you deny it to them, and then forbid them to labour, as if working less would give them more food . . . Give them liberty to work, give them the market of the world for their produce, give them the power to live comfortably, and increasing means and increasing intelligence will speedily make them independent enough and wise enough to [*limit their work*] to that point at which life shall be . . . more of recreation and enjoyment . . .'

(John Bright, speech in the House of Commons against the passing of the Factory Act, 1844)

5. (a) Why did John Bright believe that factory reform would be harmful for the factory workers themselves?
   (b) How did John Bright believe that workers would be able to improve their living and working conditions by themselves?
   (c) How did John Bright and Robert Owen differ in their attitudes to factory reform?

6. Using the sources in this section, and your own knowledge, explain why it took so long for the Ten-Hours Movement to achieve success.

Mines and Mining

Coal Production

In 1800 10,000,000 tons of coal were mined in Great Britain. This had risen to 65,000,000 tons by 1850. Why had the demand for coal increased so much? More and more coal was needed to provide the steam power to drive machinery: for example, pumps in lead, copper and coal mines, machines in textile mills and, from the 1840s, railway locomotives. More and more iron machinery was being designed and built, and the iron industry, which in the 1760s had switched from using charcoal in the smelting process to using coal, steadily increased its demand for supplies of coal.

The increasing demand for coal meant that mines were dug deeper and deeper, and life for the men, women and children working in them became more and more dangerous.

Working in the Mines

The danger began with the descent down the shafts to the coal face. Look at the picture on page 78. Once at the coal face the difficulties and dangers increased. The men and older boys usually worked as 'hewers'. They worked in narrow tunnels, often no more than 45 cm high, and cut the coal from the coal face with picks. Somehow the roof of a coal seam had to be supported as the coal was cut away. In Yorkshire and Northumberland it was usual to leave pillars of coal to do the job. The mine owners of the midlands considered this to be wasteful of good coal, and used stones or wooden pit props instead. Sometimes the stone, wood or coal which was supporting the roof collapsed; sometimes too large a gap was left between the props, and the roof fell in. Rock falls and falls of coal were common in most pits, and many miners were buried alive.

Women usually worked as 'drawers'. It was their job to move the coal, which was in trucks and attached to them by a belt and chain, from the coal face to the bottom of the shaft. In some pits the women 'drawers' only moved the coal from the coal face to the main road through the mine. There adolescent boys took over and hauled (sometimes called 'hurrying') the coal along the roads to the shaft bottom.

The work of a carrier, too, was dangerous. Carriers took the coal up the shaft to the surface by a series of ladders. The picture on page 101 shows girl carriers in a Scottish pit. One slip and the girl (or woman) carrying coal would crash to her death, and would take with her several of those behind on the ladder. By the nineteenth century, however, most coal was winched to the surface in enormous buckets.

The young children of the hewers and drawers were usually found work as 'trappers'. Most trappers were boys and girls under nine years old. Their job was to sit in a hole in the depths of the mine for hours on end, usually in the dark, and open and close the ventilation doors when trucks of coal came along.

The deeper mines became, the greater was the danger of explosions and flooding. The problem of flooding was overcome by using steam pumping engines to get rid of the water that drained into the pits. This meant, however, that pits could be dug deeper still. Deeper pits meant that dangerous gases could collect, and more and more miners were killed by explosions or were poisoned by gas.

Mines were ventilated by having several shafts cut. Sometimes a fire was lit at the bottom of one of the shafts. This sent heat up the shaft, and drew cool air down the other one. These fires, though, often caused explosive gases to ignite. The risk of explosion was cut down by the miner's safety lamp, which was invented by Humphrey Davy in 1815. This was a special lamp which gave light without letting the explosive gases come into contact with a naked flame. The flame in the lamp also turned blue whenever dangerous gases were about. The use of the miner's lamp, of course, meant that pits could be dug even deeper.

This illustration of a women coal drawer was printed in the Report of the Commission on the Employment of Women and Children in Mines and Collieries *published in 1842*

Firedamp!

Many miners were killed in accidents, and still more developed serious illnesses as a result of working in filthy conditions where the air was always thick with coal dust. The *New Statistical Account*, published in Edinburgh in 1840, stated:

'The collier population is subject to a peculiar disease called . . . the 'black spit' . . . It is a wasting of the lungs [*caused*] by the inhaling of the coal dust while working, and the expectoration [*spit*] is as black as the coal dust itself . . . Almost all the men are affected by it sooner or later, so as to be rendered unfit . . . before they drop prematurely into the grave, between the ages of 40 and 60 or 65.'

Lord Shaftesbury and the Royal Commission

Lord Shaftesbury persuaded the Prime Minister, Robert Peel (who was the son of the Robert Peel who introduced the early Factory Laws) that working conditions in the mines needed investigation. The government set up a Royal Commission in 1840 to find out what was happening, and to report on the situation.

Four Commissioners were appointed, and twenty sub-Commissioners to work under them in the various coalfields. Between 1840 and 1842 they interviewed hundreds of men, women and children. However, they couldn't visit every pit on every coalfield, and so questionnaires were sent to all mine owners. Not everyone replied, but even so the Commissioners were able to collect evidence from mine owners and from mine workers which later filled three volumes of the final Report. Lord Shaftesbury, who was the Chairman of the Commission, was not content with waiting in London to receive reports from the Commissioners and sub-Commissioners. He took an active part in the investigation, visiting several coalmines in the Black Country to see conditions for himself.

The Report of the Commission on the Employment of Women and Children in Mines and Collieries was published in 1842. It shocked those who read it. This was partly because very few people knew anything about mines or mining villages, or about the people who lived and worked there.

Mining villages were isolated and closed communities, and the people living there had very little contact with the outside world. The villages grew up around the mines, and almost all those living there would be employed by the mine owner, would rent his houses and would buy goods in his shop. In many pits, the actual mining was sub-contracted to 'butties' who were paid by the owners according to the amount of coal mined. This meant that they worked the men, women and children they employed as hard as possible – and there was no one to stop them. Mine owners were usually, also, the local magistrates, and so controlled justice in the area. The mine owners therefore had complete control over the living and working conditions of mining families. The Commissioners and sub-Commissioners uncovered stories of cruelty, danger, and terror. This began at a very early age.

Many children worked as trappers, opening and closing ventilation doors underground, as you read on page 74, usually in complete darkness. Sarah Gooder, aged eight years, told a sub-Commissioner:

> 'I'm a trapper in the Gauber Pit. I have to trap without a light and I'm scared. I go at four and sometimes half-past three in the morning, and come out at five and half past [*at night*]. I never go to sleep. Sometimes I sing when I've a light but not in the dark; I dare not sing then. I don't like being in the pit.'

Accidents to children were very common. Philip Phillips, who worked in the Plymouth mines in Merthyr Tydfil described to the sub-Commissioners what had happened to him:

> 'Nearly a year ago there was an accident and most of us were burned. I was carried home by a man. It hurt very much because all the skin was burnt off my face. I couldn't work for six months. My father is a carpenter. I have seven brothers and sisters but only five of us can find work. None of us have ever been to school.'

Many children could not stand upright whilst they were working, and they grew crooked with mis-shapen backs, arms and legs.

The conditions in which women worked were no better. Betty Harris, a woman aged thirty-seven, described to the Commissioners her work as a drawer in a coal pit in Little Bolton:

> 'I have a belt round my waist, and a chain passing between my legs, and I go on my hands and feet. The road is very steep and we have to hold by a rope . . . I am not as strong as I was and cannot stand the work so well as I used to. I have drawn till I have the skin off me; the belt and chain are worse when we are in the family way . . .'

However, most of those interviewed by the sub-Commissioners believed that mining families were, generally, better fed than those working in mills and factories. In Yorkshire a sub-Commissioner reported:

> 'The children as well as the adults, have bread and milk, or porridge, to their breakfast; huge lumps of bread, and often bits of cheese or bacon, or fat, to their luncheon in the pit; a hot meal when they come home at five or six, and often porridge, or bread and milk, or tea for supper . . . The contrast is most striking between the broad stalwart frame of the swarthy collier, as he stalks home, all grime and muscle, and the puny, pallid, starveling little weaver, with his dirty-white apron and his feminine look.'

The Mines Act 1842

Lord Shaftesbury immediately introduced a Bill to abolish all female labour in mines, along with that of pauper apprentices and boys aged under thirteen. Many mining women, however, objected to his proposal that they should be forbidden to work in the mines. Shaftesbury had no difficulty in persuading the House of Commons to listen to him. His speech intro-

A young boy pulling a sledge

Lord Shaftesbury visiting the coal mines of the Black Country, 1840–42

ducing the Bill contained little more than a summary of the Report, but even so it brought tears to the eyes of many of those MPs who were listening to him. The Bill passed the House of Commons without any trouble. This was not the case with the House of Lords. Many of the great mine owners were members of the Lords, and they were determined to oppose the Bill. They maintained that it would cost them a great deal to employ men to do the work of women and children; the cost of coal production would rise and, as coal was used in virtually every industry, British industry as a whole would suffer as a result. Lord Londonderry led the opposition, and he managed to get the clause which referred to pauper apprentices removed altogether, and to reduce from thirteen years to ten years

the age below which boys were forbidden to work in mines. He could do no more, and the Bill became law in late 1842.

The Act forbade the employment, underground, of all women and girls, and of all boys under ten years of age. Furthermore, boys under the age of fifteen were forbidden to work machinery. Later, in 1850, government Inspectors of Mines were appointed to make sure that the law was carried out.

When the Mines Act was passed, Lord Shaftesbury wrote in his diary:

'. . . Whatever has been done, it is but a millionth part of what there is to do.'

SOURCE WORK:
Coal Mining

SOURCE A

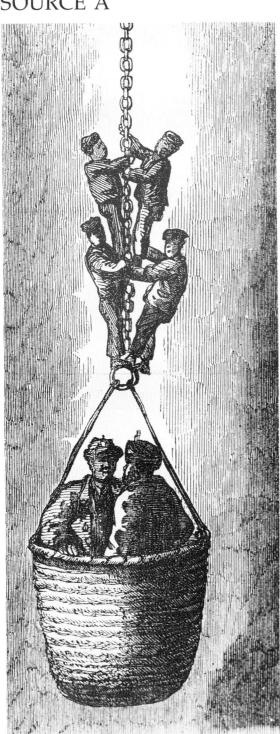

Men and boys being brought to the surface

SOURCE B

'I have been working below 3 years on my father's account: he takes me down at 2 in the morning and I come up at 1 and 2 next afternoon. I go to bed at 6 at night to be ready for work next morning. I have to bear my burden up four ladders before I get to the main road which leads to the pit bottom. My task is [*to fill*] 4 or 5 tubs. I fill 5 tubs in 20 journeys. I have had the strap when I did not do my bidding.'

(From *Parliamentary Papers (Report of the Mines Commission)*, vol. 15, 1842)

(Road = passageway underground wide enough for wagons of coal)

SOURCE C

'After I lost my light I found that I was lost and in a strange road. I could hear my father at work all Friday. I knocked the side and made as much noise as I possibly could but no one answered me. They all went out that night leaving me there. I cried very much. I thought I saw the stars two or three times although I was a hundred miles underground. I saved my dinner as much as I could, only eating a bit at a time. The whole time I had been wandering about in the dark when I heard the hauliers and made my way to them.

(From *Our Coal and Coal Pits, by a Traveller Underground*, 1853)

1. Read Sources B and C and look at A.
   (a) What particular difficulties and dangers did these children face in the mines?
   (b) In two of these sources the children say that they worked with their fathers. Would this have helped the children?
   (c) Why did the children's parents allow them to go down the mines? Use the sources in this section on coal mining and your own knowledge to help you answer this question.

2. It took three years of agitation, organisation and pressure before the Factory Act was passed in 1833. Why was it so much easier to persuade Parliament to pass the 1842 Mines Act?

Coal Mining

SOURCE D

In 1843, a year after the Mines Act was passed, the magazine *Punch* published this cartoon called 'Capital and Labour'.

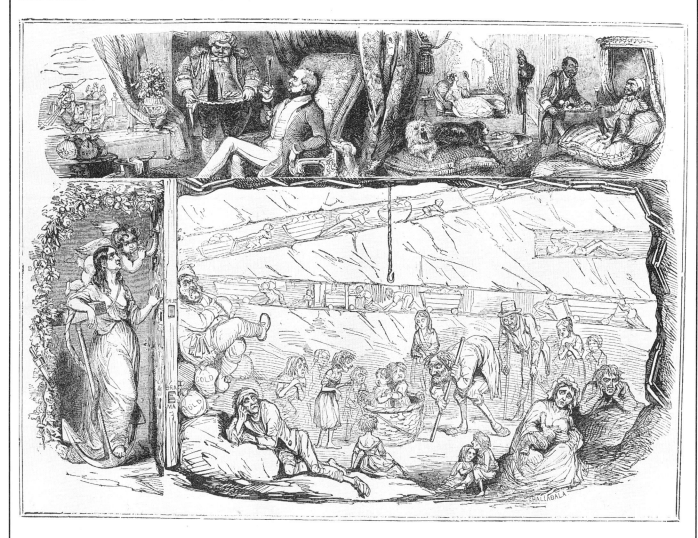

3. (a) What point was the cartoonist trying to make?
   (b) Do you think he makes his point well?
   (c) Does this mean, then, that the Mines Act had not achieved anything?

'The multitudes we see not . . .'

In 1844 Samuel Wilberforce, who was the son of William Wilberforce (see page 68) and was later to become Bishop of Oxford, wrote to the clergy of Surrey:

'We look, it may be, every Sunday, at our well filled churches, and we forget, for the moment, in the presence of those we see, the multitudes we see not; the mass behind; whom misery, as well as sin, whom want of room, want of clothes, indolence, neglect or utter wretchedness, are shutting out . . . Yet there they surely are. In all our great towns thin walls separate luxury from starvation. The two classes live in absolute ignorance of each other; there are no points of contact between them; the two streams nowhere intermingle . . .'

Churches and Churchgoing

In 1851, for the first and only time, a count was made of all the people in England and Wales who attended public worship. The date chosen for this census was Sunday, 30th March. The chart below is taken from the official report (1854) by Horace Mann, based on the *Census of Great Britain, 1851 – Religious Worship in England and Wales*:

Total population of England and Wales	17,927,609
No. of possible worshippers	12,549,326
No. of actual worshippers	7,261,032
(This includes)	
Church of England (Anglican)	3,773,474
Scottish Presbyterians	60,131
Independents	793,142
Baptists	587,978
Quakers	18,172
Wesleyan Methodists	1,385,382
Welsh Calvinistic Methodists	151,046
Roman Catholics	305,393
Mormons	18,800

On that Sunday it was discovered, as you can see, that approximately 7 million people out of a total population of approximately 18 million attended a place of worship. Of course, not all of the 18 million could have attended church even if they had wanted to. Many were small children who could only go if an adult took them; many were ill or were long-term invalids, and others were too old and infirm. Then, too, there were men and women who worked on Sundays and could not be expected to attend. When all these people were taken into account, it was reckoned that about 60 per cent of those who could have gone to a church on that Sunday did, in fact, attend. This meant, of course, that 40 per cent of those who could have attended chose not to. It was becoming clear that religion was not important to a large part of the population.

The Anglican Church

The census and Horace Mann's Report came as no surprise to many people who were closely connected with the Church of England. It confirmed what many people, among them some bishops, vicars and churchgoers, feared had been happening for many years: that the Anglican church itself, its religious services and its priests, were mainly concerned with ministering to the needs of middle-class men and women.

In 1850 John Glyde wrote a book called *The Moral, Social and Religious Condition of Ipswich*. In it he said that:

'Some of the pews for the rich were padded, lined, cushioned, and supplied with every comfort . . . The poor, on the other hand, were seated on stools in the aisles; many of the seats were without backs, to prevent the occupants from falling asleep during the sermon, and the cold, damp stone beneath their feet, was the only place to kneel during prayer . . . Some of our Church ministers of that day appeared to have fellowship only with the wealthy.'

John Glyde was writing about only one town in Suffolk, but he was describing something which was happening in many, many churches throughout Britain.

The Anglican church itself seemed to encourage the idea that the church was only supposed to be for those with money, good clothes and a position in society. To be respectable was very important to most people. The artisans, the ill and the uneducated were not considered respectable by many men and women of the middle classes – and by many ministers. The respectable classes simply did not want to mix with the labouring classes and the down-and-outs in ordinary daily life or in church.

Clothes, too, were another problem. In 1838 J.B. Sumner wrote *A Charge delivered to the Clergy of the Diocese of Chester* and pointed out that:

'Those who are in this state [*poverty*] are naturally reluctant to mingle themselves with the richer; they are unwilling to exhibit poverty and rags in contrast with wealth or splendour. The very act of attending the house of God requires of them something of an effort . . .'

Those who made this effort could well find their very poverty condemned in the sermon. This is part of one preached by the Bishop of Llandaff:

'God never meant that the idle should live upon the labour of the industrious . . . He hath therefore permitted a state of poverty to be everywhere introduced; that the industrious might enjoy the rewards of their diligence [*hard work*]; and those who would not work, might feel the punishment of their laziness.'

Many preachers believed that the poor were suffering because they were sinful. Their own wickedness had made them poor. Charity – gifts of money, clothing and food – would only help for a short time. In the end,

The Temple Church, London, in about 1830

the poor simply had to wait for death to end all their sufferings.

However, some vicars, and their bishops, were beginning to tackle the problem of 'the multitudes we see not . . .' in the growing towns of the north and midlands. From 1836 new parishes were created in these industrial areas. The vicars working in these parishes (nicknamed 'slum parsons') were nothing at all like the vicar who had some of his parishioners sitting in padded pews and others on wooden stools. The 'slum parsons' were determined to minister to the artisans and labouring classes who believed that the church was not for them.

One of these 'slum parsons' was the Rev. Walter Farquhar Hook, who was vicar of Leeds from 1837 to 1859. In 1843 he wrote to Samuel Wilberforce:

'. . . in the manufacturing districts she [*the Anglican church*] is the object of detestation to the working classes . . . The working class consider themselves to be an oppressed people . . . they consider the Church to belong to the party of their oppressors; hence they hate it . . .'

However, the Rev. Hook worked tirelessly on behalf of the artisans and paupers in Leeds. He gave his sincere support to all kinds of reform movements, like the Ten-Hours Movement (page 69), and to plans for the introduction of public parks and public education. In doing so he gained the respect of the working classes, and was known as the 'working man's vicar'.

The Rev. Walter Farquhar Hook and others like him, such as the Rev. George Stringer Bull who was vicar of Bierley, outside Bradford, and who was an active member of the Ten-Hours Movement, were determined to make Christianity relevant to the needs of people living and working in industrial towns. However, it was not only vicars who managed to show the artisans and operatives that the Anglican church did care for them. Richard Oastler (pages 68–71), for example, who was a Tory and an Anglican, campaigned long and hard against what he saw as child slavery in the mills of Yorkshire.

There were other forces for change within the Anglican church. There grew, gradually, the idea that the Church had an important part to play in the whole community. A group of Anglicans, known as Evangelicals, believed most strongly that it was their duty to take the Christian message to the labouring poor and the destitute, and to help all those who were less well-off than themselves.

Both William Wilberforce and Lord Shaftesbury, about whom you read earlier, were Evangelicals. In December 1827 Lord Shaftesbury wrote in his diary:

'Where can I be so useful as in public service? . . . I am bound to try what God has put into me for the good of old England . . . for the advancement of religion and the increase of human happiness . . .'

Bible reading

However, even the slum parson earned far more than his working-class parishioners. He was a long way away, socially, from the artisans and operatives for whom he cared. Labouring men did not become vicars, and no one ever suggested that they should. If a working-class man wanted to become involved with the organisation and control of the church, he had to look elsewhere. Many turned to Methodism.

Methodists

One of the greatest movements for reform inside the Church of England began long before the slum parsons. John Wesley (1703–91) was a Church of England clergyman. In 1729 he founded the Methodist Society, and preached the Christian gospel to miners and shopkeepers, to factory workers and farm labourers. He was often forbidden to preach in churches, and so held hundreds of outdoor services. These were usually very emotional occasions, with mass hymn singing – usually of hymns written by John's brother Charles – and plenty of dramatic preaching. On one occasion John Wesley wrote that the people:

'. . . exceedingly trembled and quaked . . . and began to call upon God with strong cries and tears . . .'

Not everyone liked what he said: sometimes he was chased out of town; sometimes he was pelted with stones.

However, very often the people listened and became converted to John Wesley's type of Christianity. Other ministers supported him, and eventually, a short time after John's death, a separate Methodist church was set up.

The influence of the Methodist church in the early nineteenth century was enormous. Many of the people who listened to Methodist preachers began to change their own lives and to become hardworking and sober. The Methodist chapels encouraged ordinary men to preach, and held regular classes at which adults discussed passages from the Bible. In this way some of the leaders of the poor were given practice at speaking in public on matters about which they cared.

Joseph Capper, a Chartist leader in the Staffordshire Potteries, was supposed to have '. . . a tongue like the sledge-hammer he used in his shop . . .' This experience was to be all important when protesting and holding meetings to gain support for such things as parliamentary reform and the right to join a trades union.

You read earlier (pages 75–6) about the Royal Commission on the Mines. One of the mine owners reported to the Commission that:

'. . . the men professing to be Methodists are the spokesmen on these occasions, and the most difficult to deal with. These men may be superior to the rest in intelligence, and generally show great skill, cunning, and circumvention . . .'

John Wesley meets an unfriendly reception in Wednesbury

Roman Catholics

In the sixteenth century the Church of England replaced the Roman Catholic church as the official national church. Ever since that time, Catholics had been hated and feared by many people. They were forbidden to hold public office, and were generally treated as outsiders. Gradually, however, the position of Catholics in Britain was changing. In 1807 Roman Catholics were allowed to vote in elections for the first time; in 1829 they were allowed to become MPs and hold important jobs in the government – but not without fierce debates in Parliament.

Gradually, more and more people felt safe in saying that they were Catholics and in joining the Catholic church. You will read in Chapter 5 about the vast numbers of Irish men, women and children who emigrated from Ireland. Most of them were Catholics, and many of them came to England. They settled in Liverpool and other industrial towns in the north, and in London.

The *Catholic Directory*, published in 1838, says that at Moorfields (part of London) four priests looked after the needs of about 30,000 Catholics. This included caring for Catholics in four charity schools, several prisons and hospitals, and no less than twenty-four workhouses. In another area of London, the *Directory* tells us that three priests:

'have daily to attend the London Hospital, Mile End Road, the receptacle of all accidents in the

docks, wharfs, and ships from Blackwall to London Bridge, as well as fifteen workhouses.'

The situation in the northern towns was the same, with Catholic priests working hard among the Catholic poor. Thomas Burke described one episode in Liverpool:

'In January 1847, the Rector of Liverpool informed the government that dysentry had assumed alarming proportions, due to the cabbages and turnips which formed the first food of the early immigrants. February saw 800 cases of typhoid; the reading of the death-toll each Sunday morning in the churches sending a cold shiver through the immense congregations . . . Then came the awful visitation of typhus. Liverpool Protestantism bowed its head in reverence at the heroism of Catholic Priests. Undaunted, they went from room to room in crowded houses; from cellar to garret, ministering to the sick . . .'

Not all the men and women who worked tirelessly to help the poor were inspired to do so by their religious beliefs. Many were simply shocked and horrified by the conditions in which the poor lived and worked, and it was this which drove them to try to bring about change. Others, however, as you have seen, were driven by their religious beliefs to help the poor, the homeless and the down-and-outs.

SOURCE WORK:
Religion and Poverty

SOURCE A

Christmas at church

SOURCE B

One of the most well-known hymns written in the nineteenth century was 'All things bright and beautiful', which Mrs Alexander wrote in 1848. This is one of the verses:

> The rich man in his castle
>   The poor man at his gate
> God made them, high or lowly
>   And order'd their estate.

SOURCE C

The Rev. T. Thorp, a minister in the Anglican Church, was the author of a book called *Individual Vice, Social Sin*, which was published in 1832. In it he wrote:

'. . . For these things does my heart fail within me when I see in the poor, no marks of deference [*respect*] for the rich, in the ignorant none of submission to the wise, in the labourer none of attachment to his employer . . .'

1. (a) What does the illustration (Source A) tell you about the Anglican church in the nineteenth century?
   (b) What does the hymn (Source B) say about wealth and poverty?
   (c) Now read Source C. Do these sources, taken together, help to explain why many working-class people did not go to church?

SOURCE D

You read on page 30 about Chartists and religion. This is an extract from a Chartist circular, printed in November 1839, which explains what some Chartists believed was happening in the churches:

'In the school and the church, the people are taught that passive obedience is a virtue – that faith is paramount to [*more important than*] knowledge . . . They are taught to believe that they are mercifully created to endure poverty, and that the rich are very unfortunate in being born to the care and trouble of ruling over the poor. They are also taught that God created them poor, for the salvation of their immortal souls; and that through tribulation [*troubles*] they must enter Heaven. . .'

2. (a) What does this Chartist circular say about the ways in which the church behaved towards the poor?
   (b) Look back at the section *The Anglican Church*. What evidence can you find which supports what the Chartist circular says?
   (c) Did all churches and churchmen treat the labouring poor in the ways described in the Chartist circular? Remember to back up your answer with evidence.

Religion and Poverty

3. Explain carefully how the following groups of people helped the artisans, factory operatives and paupers in the cities and towns of the industrial north and midlands: (i) Slum parsons; (ii) Methodist preachers; (iii) Roman Catholic priests.

SOURCE E

Lord Shaftesbury visiting the slums of London, 1840

4. It was not usual for members of the aristocracy to visit slum areas. Use your knowledge to explain why Lord Shaftesbury would bother to make visits like this.

5. Why did Lord Shaftesbury work so hard to improve the living and working conditions of the labouring poor? Was it because of his religious beliefs, or because of what he saw and heard when he went down the mines and visited the slums?

Law and Order

Execution at Tyburn

This picture was drawn by William Hogarth in 1747. The people certainly seem to have turned the public hanging of a criminal into a festive occasion. If you look carefully you can see refreshments being sold; people jostling each other to get a better view; a couple of fights starting; a woman selling news-sheets and a man releasing a carrier pigeon. All public hangings were regarded by most people as a good excuse for a holiday and a bit of fun. This had been the case when, for example, the rogue Jonathan Wild had been executed at Tyburn in 1725 for organising armed gangs in London. It was the same, too, when the butcher's apprentice Dick Turpin, who turned poacher, thief, robber, highwayman and murderer, was finally hanged at York in 1739.

By the 1770s over 200 crimes were punishable by death. These ranged from stealing from a shop goods which were worth five shillings or more, to murder. However, only a relatively small number of executions were actually carried out. Usually only forgers, riot leaders and murderers were hanged. Judges gradually became reluctant to sentence people to death for what they had begun to believe were relatively minor offences. About two thirds of all prisoners were sentenced to transportation. To these were added those who should by law have been hanged, but who had had their sentence changed to one of transportation. Up until the

1780s men, women and children were transported in convict ships to America. After the American War of Independence (1775–83) the convict ships sailed to Australia and other colonies instead.

Death and transportation were punishments for what were considered to be the more serious crimes. Relatively few criminals were sent to prison: most were whipped, put in the local pillory or fined. About half of the people who were in prison were there because they could not pay their debts. The rest were robbers, thieves, prostitutes or vagabonds.

Convict Hulks

As soon as it became clear, during the American War of Independence, that convicts could no longer be transported to America, the government took action. The convicts who would have been sent to America had to be imprisoned somewhere. Large wooden warships were beached at Woolwich, Portsmouth and Chatham. They were stripped of their guns, and equipped so that they would each hold hundreds of prisoners. They were quickly filled. Even when transportation began again, but to Australia, Tasmania, Gibralter and Bermuda, the hulks were still overcrowded. Convicts sentenced to up to seven years' transportation usually only travelled as far as one of the hulks where they remained until the end of their sentence. Men convicted of serious crimes which needed to be punished by a long term of imprisonment usually ended up, too, in one of these convict hulks.

A Select Committee of the House of Commons investigated hulks and prisons in 1831–2. This is part of their report on the hulks:

'The convicts, after being shut up for the night are allowed to have lights between decks, in some ships as late as ten o'clock . . . they are permitted the use of musical instruments; . . . dancing, fighting and gaming take place; the old offenders are in the habit of robbing the newcomers; . . . a communication is frequently kept up with their old associates on shore; and occasionally spirits are introduced on board . . .'

Fifteen years later nothing seemed to have changed. A group of MPs visited five hulks which were anchored at Woolwich. They reported that:

'. . . The men sleep in hammocks. Prisoners work in the dockyards. In the hospital ship *Unite* the great majority of the patients were infested with vermin and their persons begrimed with dirt, many men had been five weeks without a change, all record had been lost of when the blankets had been washed. A large proportion of the convicts were affected by symptoms of scurvy. Convicts have been whipped with a birch without reference to the Superintendent . . .'

In the same report, the MPs recorded the convicts' duties:

'. . . At 3.30am the Quartermaster, accompanied by a Guard, is to unlock the cell where the cooks are confined and let them up to prepare breakfast. At 5.0am all hands are to be called, the hammocks lowered and made up. At 6.0 breakfast to be served, at 6.30 wards to be swept.

At 7.0 prisoners mustered out to labour in gangs, irons to be examined, and prisoners to be searched. At quarter before 12 prisoners are to return on board and be searched, dinner served. At 1.0 the prisoners are to be mustered to labour, searched, and at quarter before 6.0 they return. Each prisoner after washing himself to take his hammock and proceed to his ward. Supper to be served and cells locked. After prayers prisoners may be allowed to write to their friends . . .'

In the 1830s the people who administered colonies like Australia, to which prisoners who were actually transported were sent, began to protest. They wanted to attract men and women who genuinely wished to settle; they wanted people who would work hard to make the colony prosperous. They were no longer prepared to take an endless stream of convicts. Transportation was stopped in stages, and ended finally in 1853.

The change-over from transportation to imprisonment as a punishment was gradual one. The American

Prisoners in a prison ship

War of Independence meant that judges had to find alternative kinds of punishment. When transportation again became possible, many judges chose not to use it as a punishment, but carried on sending people to gaols instead. By the 1820s it was more usual for a convict to be sent to gaol than it was for one to be transported. The ideas of people like Elizabeth Fry, whom you will read about in a later section, supported those who preferred to see prisoners in gaols rather than transported. New prisons, like Dartmoor in Devon and Parkhurst on the Isle of Wight, were built to take the convicts who could not be sent overseas. Dartmoor, in particular, provided a harsh regime for the more desperate criminals.

Gaols, Gaol-Keepers and Turnkeys

Even before the building of new prisons, the hulks could not hold all the prisoners who were convicted and sentenced to imprisonment. More and more convicts were sent to gaols, lock-ups and bridewells (places of correction) in towns and cities. Sometimes these prisons were purpose-built, like Newgate in London; often they were old castles and toll-booths. Some buildings were so ramshackle that the prisoners had to be chained to the floors or weighed down with leg-irons to stop them escaping; all were filthy and disease ridden, and most prisoners were at the mercy of their gaolers who were usually corrupt. Most gaol-keepers and their assistants, the turnkeys, were unpaid. They could only make a living by offering better accommodation to those prisoners who could afford to pay for it, and by charging a levy on all prisoners before they would release them.

Elizabeth Fry (1780–1845)

Elizabeth Fry's family belonged to the Society of Friends – often known as the Quakers. Quakers believe that, for them, Christian sacraments such as baptism and the Eucharist are not important. Far more important in bringing man closer to God is what they call the 'inner light' of Jesus Christ in the soul. For Quakers, worship in their meeting houses is usually silent, with men and women speaking only if they feel moved to do so. Many Quakers, because of their belief in the 'inner light' in the souls of every man, woman and child, became involved in social reform movements.

Elizabeth Fry's father, John Gurney, was a Norwich banker. Although the family were Quakers, the Gurney children were not brought up in a strict, religious discipline. Nevertheless, when Elizabeth was about eighteen years old, her sister Catherine noticed a change in her. The following comment by Catherine is noted in G. King Lewis's book *Elizabeth Fry*, which was published in 1910:

'. . . A change became daily more evident in her . . . When she told me she could no longer dance with us any more it was almost more than I could bear, and I tried to argue with her, and begged and persecuted her. But it was all in vain. The

firmness of her character was now called into play and I never remember her to have been shaken in one single point which she felt to be her duty. The Bible became her study, visiting the poor, especially the sick, her great object . . .'

When she was twenty, reluctantly, Elizabeth married a wealthy London banker, Joseph Fry. Her marriage was to take her away from the free school for poor children which she had started. It was, however, after she had been married for thirteen years that she began to become involved in what was to be her life's work. An American Quaker visited the Fry household. Their visitor told Elizabeth about the terrible conditions in which women prisoners were living in Newgate prison. Not only was there great overcrowding, but few of the women had proper beds and were forced to sleep on dirty straw. There were no medicines and no doctors, and a great deal of fighting and drunkenness. Horrified, Elizabeth Fry and her friends took bundles of clean straw to the prison, and clothes for the prisoners' children. Later, she managed to visit the women's section. One of her supporters, Thomas Buxton, who wrote a book, published in 1818, called *An Enquiry whether Crime and Misery are Produced or Prevented by the Prison System* described her first visit:

'. . . Nearly three hundred women, sent there for every gradation of crime, some untried, and some under sentence of death, were crowded together in the two wards and two cells . . . They slept on the floor, at times one hundred and twenty in one ward, without so much as a mat for bedding; and many of them were nearly naked. She saw them openly drinking spirits . . . . Everything was filthy to excess, and the smell was quite disgusting . . .'

Elizabeth Fry never forgot the scenes she saw in Newgate prison. For the next few years she was busy with her growing family of ten children. However, in 1817 she was back again at Newgate. She wrote in her journal:

'. . . It was more like a slave ship. The begging, swearing, gaming, fighting, singing, dancing, dressing up in men's clothes were too bad to be described. . . '

After two more visits, Elizabeth was committed to trying to improve the lives of the women prisoners and their children. She wrote in her journal:

'Third Month, 7th 1817
My mind and time have been much taken up with Newgate and its concerns . . . May I . . . be enabled to keep my eye singly unto the Lord, that what I do may be done heartily unto Him, and not, in any degree, unto man.'

Elizabeth Fry worked hard inside Newgate. She organised a school for the children, and persuaded the prison governor to agree to changes in the women's routine: they were to have a female warder; they were to be taught useful skills like sewing, and they were to wear plain, sensible uniforms. A visitor to Newgate

This picture shows Elizabeth Fry working with women prisoners at Newgate prison

wrote about the changes which he saw:

'The courtyard, into which I was admitted, instead of being peopled with beings scarcely human, blaspheming, fighting, tearing each other's hair or gaming with a filthy pack of cards for the very clothes they wore (which often did not suffice even for decency) presented a scene where stillness and prosperity reigned . . . At the head of a long table sat a lady belonging to the Society of Friends. She was reading aloud to about sixteen women prisoners, who were engaged in needlework around it. Each wore a clean looking apron and bib . . . They all rose at my entrance, curtsied respectfully, and then at a signal given, resumed their seats and their employment.'

Elizabeth Fry formed a Ladies' Association for the Improvement of Female Prisoners in Newgate, which was to monitor conditions in Newgate, and recommend improvements. This Committee continued her work in Newgate while she extended her work to other prisons. With her brother Joseph she travelled the country, visiting prisons wherever they went. Joseph made the reason for their journeys clear:

'The principal object of our journey was connected with the concerns of our own religious society, that of Friends; but we also made a point of inspecting the prisons in the several towns through which we passed . . . and I think it right to communicate to the public the information which we collected, in the hope that it may afford some fresh stimulous, to the zeal already prevalent for improving our system of prison discipline . . .'

Reports on many other such visits followed, and were published. Many important and influential people, like Lord Sidmouth who was Home Secretary between 1812 and 1822, were not impressed by her work. They believed that nothing was achieved by 'soft' methods. Sir Robert Peel, however, disagreed. He was to follow Lord Sidmouth as Home Secretary and, as you will see, took a very different attitude to prison reform.

Elizabeth Fry died in 1845 when she was sixty-five years old. An obituary in the *Illustrated London News* said of her work:

'Her whole life was one continued course of active exertion, which has been attended with many beneficial results. She gave much attention to the condition of female convicts and prisoners, at a time when our prison discipline and management were many degrees worse than they are now. Her efforts secured her the respect of all Christians, and acquired for her name European reputation.'

Elizabeth Fry wanted prisons to be more disciplined and ordered. She wanted criminals to be punished, but

The treadmill and oakum shed, Holloway Prison, in about 1850

she also wanted them to learn new ways of living through the work which they were given to do whilst they were in prison. However, some prisons became even more repressive than Elizabeth Fry could have imagined. Pentonville prison in London, for example, tried to keep its prisoners separated from each other. It was believed that if a man was separated from his evil companions, then he would be more likely to turn to right ways of living when he was released.

Prisoners were given work to do, but it was monotonous – and some of it was pointless. It would hardly fit them for a better life once they were released. The illustration above shows prisoners in Holloway prison. Not only are they isolated from each other by the small cells in which they sit, but the work they are doing is very boring. They are picking oakum – untwisting the tarred ropes used on ships. The men to the top right of the picture are walking a treadmill. They stand in a framework, and 'walk' continuously on wooden steps which are fixed to a cylinder. The walking makes the cylinder revolve. Some treadmills were used to pump water or to grind corn. Others were connected to nothing at all, and served simply to keep the prisoners occupied.

The Death Penalty and Prisons: Parliament Acts

Sir Robert Peel (1788–1850), as you have read, became Home Secretary in 1822. He was then thirty-four years

old, and a promising Tory politician. Unlike Lord Sidmouth, who had been Home Secretary before him, Robert Peel was influenced by the ideas of reformers like Elizabeth Fry. He also had to find hundreds more prison places as more and more convicts were sentenced to prison instead of transportation.

At the beginning of the nineteenth century Sir Samuel Romilly had led a campaign to remove the death penalty from a whole number of offences. His proposals had, in the end, been defeated by the House of Lords. Peel, however, was working at a time when the ideas of many people had changed. He also thought it important that the law matched the actual sentencing which judges were doing. Most were becoming reluctant to sentence people to death for what were seen as relatively minor offences. In 1823 Peel managed to persuade Parliament to agree to abolish the death penalty for about 100 crimes. It was removed from still more crimes in the 1830s, and after 1837 the death penalty was only used for the crimes of murder and treason. The last public hanging took place in 1868.

The Prison Act of 1823 made it possible for gaol-keepers and turnkeys to be paid wages, and forbade them to take fees from their prisoners. At the same time the Act stated that women prisoners had to have women gaol-keepers. It was not, however, until 1835 that the first prison inspectors were appointed. Prisons, however, were still, in the words of the 1823 Prison Act, to be 'objects of terror' to all lawbreakers.

Parish Constables and Watchmen

It had been the responsibility of every parish, from the Middle Ages, to appoint a parish constable. By the beginning of the nineteenth century parish constables were appointed each year by the local magistrate. The constable's job was part-time and unpaid. This system worked well in small rural parishes where a constable might have to leave his regular job, say, four or five times a year to catch a sheep stealer or a pickpocket at the local market.

Towns like London, which were made up of many parishes and where there was a great deal of crime, simply could not cope. The smarter parishes employed watchmen as well as using the unpaid constables. However, watchmen's wages were low and they were often elderly. Some watchmen were made fun of, and they were nicknamed 'Charlies'. A watchman would stand in his watch-box and look out for anyone attempting anything criminal. Most watchmen carried a rattle to raise the alarm if they did see anything suspicious.

The Fielding Brothers and the Bow Street Runners

In the early eighteenth century, criminals could only be arrested if they were caught in the act of committing a crime, or if they were informed upon. Tracking down criminals was the responsibility of the magistrates.

Henry Fielding and his half-brother John were both magistrates at Bow Street Magistrates Court, London. They created a force of men, the Bow Street Runners, who pursued criminals and searched for stolen goods. By 1800 London had teams of 'Runners' working from eight magistrates' courts.

Sir Robert Peel, Peelers and Bobbies

In 1822, when Sir Robert Peel became Home Secretary, just over one million people lived in London. Yet London had only just over 5,000 constables, watchmen and runners to cope with the crime and disorder in the capital city. Too often troops had to be called in to deal with disturbances, and they usually made a bad situation worse. It took Peel until 1829 to persuade Parliament that a single, united, trained police force was the only way of combatting crime.

In 1829 Parliament passed the Metropolitan Police Act. Within a few months 3,000 policemen, nicknamed 'Peelers' or 'Bobbies' after Sir Robert Peel, were patrolling the streets of London. It was important that people did not think of them as soldiers. The new police uniform was therefore blue. Every policeman wore a long-tailed coat over his trousers, and a tall hat which was specially strengthened. The police, unlike soldiers, did not carry guns. Each policeman carried a truncheon and a wooden rattle with which to sound a warning. All policemen were paid a wage, and had to be able to read, write and do simple arithmetic.

Although the police did not look like soldiers, they were organised on military lines. The new Force was

A Peeler

divided into divisions and planned like an army, with superintendents, inspectors, sergeants and constables.

The Metropolitan Police Force acted as a model for all other police forces. The Municipal Corporations Act of 1835 (see page 60) required all boroughs to appoint a Watch Committee. These Watch Committees were responsible for forming their own borough police forces. By 1848 only 22 of the 171 boroughs in England and Wales were still without police. Justices of the Peace in the counties were allowed, by an Act of Parliament in 1836, to set up a paid police force if they thought one was neccessary. Twenty years later they were forced by law to establish a police force if they had not already done so.

SOURCE WORK:
Law and Order

SOURCE A

Preparing for an execution outside Newgate

1. Look carefully at Source A, which was drawn in 1848.
   (a) Describe the behaviour of the crowd.
   (b) Now look at the picture on page 86, which was drawn in 1747.
       In what ways is the behaviour of the crowd, shown here, similar to that of the crowd in Source A?
   (c) Re-read the section on page 90, *The Death Penalty and Prisons: Parliament Acts*. One of the reasons why Robert Peel was able to persuade Parliament to abolish the death penalty for so many crimes was that people's ideas as to what should be punishable by death were changing.
       Are you, then, surprised that the crowds watching an execution in 1747 should behave in very similar ways to the crowds watching an execution in 1848? Give reasons for your answer.

SOURCE B

Richard Taylor was a convict who was transported to Australia. In 1851 he wrote home to his father in England. His letter is now kept in the Lancashire Record Office. This is part of what he wrote:

'. . . I was assigned to the Hospital where I had 39 fellows one of whom was a boot and shoe maker and I eventually picked up the trade by which I earn a comfortable living. I live in my little property, it is only half an acre but it faces the road where the gold coach passes. I married my wife when she was a fellow 'servant', two of my children goes to school every day. Tell my brother good tradesmen can earn from one to two guineas a week and provisions are much cheaper here, this is the land of plenty and perpetual summer . . .

2. What was the driving force which inspired Elizabeth Fry to help women prisoners at Newgate: her pity for the women she saw there, or her desire to serve God?
   Remember to back up your answer with evidence.

3. Read Source B carefully. Does this mean that all convicts would have preferred transportation to imprisonment in England?
   Use the sources and the information on pages 86–8 to support your answer.

Law and Order

SOURCE C

Every prison and convict hulk had to send information about their prisoners to the Home Office. This source is part of the quarterly return from Portland Prison, and was made in 1849.

Name	Age	Offence	Where	Sentence
James Hackett	21	Felony	Salford	7
John Taylor	20	Stealing file & monies	Leicester	7
John Brown	20	Larceny previous con.	C.C. Court	7
James Barker	47	Stealing fowls, 2 indicts.	Exeter	14
William Johnson	25	Setting fire to 2 stacks of straw	Stafford	20
James Sweeny	58	Uttering count coin P.C.	Caernarvon	15
George Williams	21	Burglary P.C.	C.C. Court	10
Francis Best	35	Housebreaking & Larceny	Worcester	15
John Henry	36	Uttering forged notes	Glasgow	20
Thomas Hartshorn	33	Robbery with violence P.C.	Liverpool	15
Samuel Laughton	22	Burglary, stealing silver spoons etc.	Nottingham	14
Thomas Robinson	23	Burglary and theft, 2 indict.	Maidstone	14
Martin Stone	22	House stealing	Dorchester	15
Richard Ashford	58	Stealing 3lbs of pork P.C.	Exeter	14
John Dobson	28	Stealing money from the parson P.C.	Stafford	14
Samuel Diggle	36	Burglary	Liverpool	15
George Goult	22	Robbery P.C.	Chelmsford	12
Robert Holder	23	Stealing from a dwelling £15 & Pr pistols	Portsmouth	15
Richard Jones	36	Warehouse breaking and stealing malt and hops	Reading	15
Hugh King alias Cameron	36	Theft by housebreaking	Glasgow	14
Austin Montroe	34	Larceny in a dwelling to the value of £5 P.C.	C.C. Court	15

4. The sentence given to a particular crime usually reflects the seriousness of that crime.
   (a) List all the crimes given in the source, in order of length of sentence.
      Put the crimes with the longest sentence at the top of your list.
   (b) What conclusions can you draw about the types of crimes which were regarded as being the most serious in the 1830s and 1840s?
   (c) Using your knowledge of the period, suggest reasons for this.
   (d) What else could an historian discover from this source?

P.C. = previous conviction
indict. = indictment
C. C. Court = Central Criminal Court, London
larceny = theft

SOURCE D

This is an extract from a local newspaper, the *Aylesbury News*, and was published in 1839.

'At Chesham there is a smith appointed constable, thief-taker and peace officer who has been publicly flogged in the town of Chesham, once privately flogged at Aylesbury Gaol, once convicted of stealing lead, and once committed to hard labour for assaulting and robbing a boy.'

5. Read Source D carefully, and check back with the information on page 91.
   (a) Would the constable described in this newspaper report be more likely to be one of the new 'Peelers' or 'Bobbies', or one of the older style parish constables?
      Explain your answer carefully.
   (b) How does Source D help to explain why a national police force was needed?

6. Important reforms were made in the 1820s and 1830s in the sorts of punishments prisoners would receive if they were found guilty, and the ways in which criminals were treated. Why was it possible to make these reforms at that time, and not before?

Schools and Schooling

There were many kinds of schools in Britain in the nineteenth century. They gave very different kinds of education to the children of the aristocrats, the gentry, the industrialists and manufacturers, shopkeepers and the labouring poor.

The Aristocracy, Gentry and Middle Classes

The sons and daughters of the landed gentry and aristocracy were taught basic reading and writing at home by governesses when they were very young. Then, because boys and girls were expected to have different accomplishments and behave differently in adult life, they were taught separately. The boys would be taught Greek and Latin, mathematics and French by a tutor. Sometimes they would be sent away to board at one of the great public schools, like Charterhouse, Rugby or Eton. This sort of education, it was thought, would turn the boys into cultured gentlemen and equip them to play their part in upper-class society. They would be able to supervise the management of their estates, become magistrates or Members of Parliament, enter the civil service or become officers in the British army.

For the girls it was different. They needed to grow into young ladies who would make good marriages with young men from similar, or more wealthy, homes. In order, then, for a girl to become properly educated, she needed to be taught certain skills. She needed to learn how to keep household accounts and how to manage servants. She needed to have certain accomplishments: music, painting, dancing and embroidery were all important in the part she had to play as a wife and mother. Where these skills could not be taught by the governess, the girl's parents would hire, for example, a drawing master who would teach a certain number of lessons a week. Sometimes the boys' tutor would teach the girls a little French conversation.

Local businessmen, lawyers, doctors and factory owners could send their sons to the local grammar school. Many towns had their own grammar schools, and some of these dated back to the middle ages. Most of these schools had ancient statutes which laid down what was to be taught – usually Latin and Greek – and provided money which was invested to pay the schoolmaster's salary. Often these schools had been founded to give a free education to the sons of special groups of people, such as guildmen.

Towards the end of the eighteenth century some of these schools began to change in order to provide a more suitable education for the boys whose parents wanted them to enter business and commerce. Macclesfield Grammar School, for example, began to teach writing, arithmetic, geography, navigation, mathematics and French. The school became so popular that,

A sketch of Charterhouse School published in the Illustrated London News *in 1800*

The Free Grammer School in Tamworth, drawn in 1829

in the early nineteenth century, sons of the neighbouring aristocracy and gentry were sent there as well as the sons of the merchants and industrialists in nearby towns. However, the majority of grammar schools did not change their curriculum to meet new demands from parents and business.

By the 1830s many middle-class parents were becoming dissatisfied with the sort of education which was offered by their local grammar schools, and began looking elsewhere. They started to send their sons to the new dissenting academies. These were private schools which had come into existence after 1779 when Protestant non-conformists were allowed, for the first time, to become teachers. These dissenting academies taught a wide range of subjects in a lively and interesting way. Hazelwood School in Birmingham, for example, provided a wide range of subjects from which pupils could choose which they wanted to study; pupils were taught in sets according to their ability, not classes according to their age; the whole school was very carefully organised, and the pupils were encouraged to become actively involved in lessons. It was schools like these which were attractive to the middle-class bankers and factory managers, and which threatened the existence of the old grammar schools.

The range of schools available to middle-class parents grew and grew. The *Quartery Journal of Education* (Vol.1,

No. 2) published in April 1831 reported on the number of new 'proprietary' schools which were being founded. Many parents, the journal reported, thought it better ' to found a school, and make it good, than run the doubtful chance of placing their sons where they may learn nothing to any purpose.' The Liverpool Institute (1825) was the first of these schools. It was soon followed by many others, some of which quickly became an important part of the towns they served. In 1837, for example, the 'Proprietary School for the Town and County of Leicester' was set up. It was backed by a group of local businessmen, tradesmen and manufacturers who controlled the city after the 1835 Municipal Corporations Act (see page 60). This particular school had an imposing building, paid the headmaster a good salary (£500 a year) and concentrated on teaching 'relevant' subjects.

Many girls from wealthy homes, as you read earlier, spent their time at home, being educated by governesses and the occasional tutor. Others, particularly the daughters of middle-class families (for example doctors, factory managers and shopkeepers) went to a variety of academies and private schools. Some of these were opened for a particular purpose, like the school which was opened in 1815 in order to teach the daughters of officers killed in the Napoleonic wars how to earn their own living. Others were opened simply in response to local demand for schools which would teach girls the knowledge and skills their parents believed they would need in adult life.

In 1834 the Manchester Statistical Society made a survey of local 'superior private and boarding schools'. They discovered that the borough of Manchester had 114 such schools, thirty-six of which were for the education of boys, and seventy-eight for the education of girls. Eighty-nine of these schools had been established since 1820, and most were run by dissenters. As well as reading and writing, they taught the girls history, geography, French, drawing, music and some arithmetic. What was happening in Manchester was happening in other towns and cities throughout the country. Not all these schools, however, were good schools.

None of the children educated by tutors or governors, in public schools, grammar schools, proprietary schools or dissenting academies were the children of the labouring poor.

The children of the Labouring Poor

Many children did not go to any kind of school at all. Indeed, it was not until 1880 that Parliament made it compulsory for every child under the age of ten to attend school. Most of the children who did not go to school before 1880 were the children of the labouring poor. They worked in mines, mills and factories, and the money these children earned was usually desperately needed by their families. There were, however, some schools for the children of the labouring poor. Whether a girl or boy attended them, though, depended upon whether such a school existed within walking distance of his or her home; whether the parents could afford the fee, or could afford for the child not to be working; and whether the parents placed any sort of importance at all upon their children being able to read and write.

Dame Schools

Many of those who did go to school went to 'dame schools' like the one illustrated below. Most dame schools were for infants only. These schools were usually run by elderly women in their own homes in order to provide themselves with a small income. Some 'dames' did their best to teach basic reading and even some writing; most were little more than child-minders. The problem was, of course, that dame schools charged around four pence a week for each pupil, which was way beyond the means of many parents.

Common Day-schools

Older children could, if their parents could afford it, go on from a dame school to a common day-school. Parents who could afford to pay nine pence a week or more were able to send their children to common day-schools which were able to provide teaching in basic subjects as well as reading, writing and arithmetic. This kind of education usually fitted their children to become, for example, clerks and shop assistants.

A dame school in Camden Town in the 1850s

SOURCE WORK:
Emigration

SOURCE A

In 1836 a book by George Cornewall Lewis was published in London. It was called *On Local Disturbances in Ireland, and on the Irish Church Question.* This is part of what the author had to say about evictions in Ireland:

'It often happens that the landlord, at the ending of a lease, finds thirty or forty tenants, and as many mud cabins, instead of the one tenant to whom the farm was originally let. What is a landlord . . . to do? Either he must surrender to the evil . . . or he must set about clearing his estate . . . Now there are only two ways in which a landlord can set about clearing the estate; he may buy out tenants . . . or he may forcibly eject them, and throw down their cabins . . .'

SOURCE B

1. Read Source A.
   (a) What problems, according to Source A, did an Irish landlord face in trying to make a living from renting out land?
   Now look at Source B.
   (b) How does Source A help to explain what is happening in Source B?

2. Look carefully at Source B.
   The people are very poor, and clearly do not make a good living from the land.
   Why, then, are they pleading to be allowed to stay? Use your understanding of events in Ireland at this time to help you explain your answer.

SOURCE C

In 1820 a book called *An Account of the Improvements on the Estates of the Marquess of Stafford* was published. It was written by James Loch, the land agent whom you read about on page 105. In this extract, James Loch explains about the benefits which the Highland Clearances will bring:

'The adoption of the new system, by which mountainous districts are converted into sheep pastures . . . is advantageous to the Scottish nation at large. The effect of this change is most advantageous to the Highlanders themselves . . . The 'Improvements' have had constantly for their aim the employment, the comfort and happiness of every individual who has been removed . . . and to benefit those to whom these extensive lands belonged.'

3. Whom, according to James Loch, were the Clearances intended to benefit?

4. Is James Loch's account of the Scottish Clearances biased? Use the information and evidence in the section on Scottish emigration to help you explain your answer.

SOURCE D

In 1963, 170 years after the Highland Clearances, John Prebble wrote a book about them called *The Highland Clearances.* This is part of what has to say about what happened to some of the families who were evicted from Sutherland:

'Some Highlanders were sent to the bitter rocky stretch between the mouth of the river Naver and Strathy Point . . . where there is no safe harbour, where the wind came without interruption from the Arctic Circle, and where men were expected to live on what an inhuman sea chose to offer them . . . William Mackay was sucked away by the waves while inspecting his little lot while his wife and children watched. John Campbell was drowned in the same way. Bell Mackay, a married woman, was taken by the sea while making salt . . . Robert Mackay fell and was killed while collecting plovers' eggs for his starving family . . . John MacDonald, while fishing, was swept off rocks and never seen again . . .'

5. This account would seem to conflict with what James Loch said happened to the Highlanders who were evicted (Source C).
   How would you explain this apparent contradiction?

Emigration

SOURCE E

'They Have Been Driven Away, To America Across the Sea'

6. Look carefully at Source E, and then look back to Source B.
   One shows an eviction in the Highlands of Scotland, the other shows an eviction in Ireland.
   These pictures of the evictions seem very similar. Does this mean that the *reasons* for the evictions must have been the same? Explain your answer.

7. Everything listed below has some connection with emigration:

   (i)   the discovery of gold in California and Australia;
   (ii)   potato blight;
   (iii) new shipping routes;
   (iv)   free passages;
   (v)   the poor-rate;
   (vi)   Great Cheviot sheep;
   (vii) emigration committees.

   (a) Explain the part played by each one in the emigration of people from Britain during the first half of the nineteenth century.
   (b) Look back at the list. Is any one more important than any of the others in explaining the increase in emigration at this time?

SOURCE F

Ford Madox Brown was a painter who travelled Europe as a young man. He returned to live in England in 1845, when he was twenty-four years old. This is his most famous painting, which was finished in 1855. It is called *The Last of England*. He decided to paint this picture after a friend, the artist Thomas Woolner, had emigrated to Australia in 1852. Ford Madox Brown used his wife Emma and himself as models from which to paint the two adults in the picture.

8. Look carefully at this picture by Ford Madox Brown.
   (a) How likely was it that emigrants from England would have looked like the people in this picture? Use the information and sources in this chapter to explain your answer.
   (b) This picture was very popular in the middle of the nineteenth century. Copies hung in many middle-class homes. Use your knowledge of the time to explain why.

6

RAILWAYS

In 1815 there were no railways linking cities and towns, ports and mines. Heavy goods were carried by sea or by canal. Rich and well-to-do people travelled by coach or private carriage. Those who were not quite so well-off could travel by stage-coach. A network of stage-coach services covered most of the major routes in the country, and a journey from, say, London to Newcastle would cost a few pounds. Those who could not begin to think of spending this sort of money would go by stage-wagon. These were huge, lumbering wooden-wheeled wagons pulled by a team of horses. They carried parcels, packages and people around the countryside cheaply – and slowly. Those who could not afford a stage-wagon just walked. Yet, by 1851 long-distance coach travel was over, and many canal companies had been forced out of business; thousands of poor people from the north and the midlands had visited London for the first time, and thousands more had had their first glimpse of the sea.

This had happened, quite simply, because of the railway. By 1851 nearly 7,000 miles of track had been laid, linking all Britain's major towns and ports. Over 67 million passenger journeys were made in 1851, and approximately 50 million tons of freight were carried by rail. Yet no one person, or group of people, sat down and designed the new transport system. The story of this transport revolution is the story of genius and hard work, of skill and daring, and of corruption and greed.

The First Railways

The very first railways were simply wooden tracks laid down to carry horse-drawn wagons of coal. It was clearly easier for a horse to pull heavy cart-loads if the wheels of the cart were not sinking into wet, muddy ground, or if the cart itself was not being overturned because the wheels hit rocks or stones, or got stuck in

A Newcastle wagon, 1773

potholes. It was a long time before anyone thought of replacing the horse with another sort of power – the steam engine. It is important to understand that there were two strands to the early development of railways. One of the strands was the track – the rails on which the wagons ran. The other strand was the locomotion – the power which made the wagons move.

Track

The earliest wooden railways were used in the Wollaton colliery, Nottinghamshire, in the first half of the seventeenth century. Their use quickly spread to wherever heavy loads had to be moved, for example to other coal mines and to iron works. However, wood easily wore down, and would split and break if it became dry or if the load passing over it was too heavy. The developing iron industry meant that iron was more readily available – and fairly cheap. Iron plates were therefore fastened onto the wooden rails to strengthen them. Gradually, however, iron replaced the wood altogether, and from 1760 iron rails became common. At first cast-iron was used. However, this did break rather easily. In 1820 John Birkinshaw, from Bedlington in Northumberland, used the newly developed wrought iron to make much stronger rails.

There were problems in keeping an iron (or wooden) wheel on an iron rail. It was all too easy for the wheel to slip off. In 1767 Richard Reynolds developed a flanged rail – a rail with a lip which would hold the wheel. Later the flange was moved from the rail to the wheel.

By the early years of the nineteenth century, then, rails had been developed which were long lasting and capable of carrying very heavy loads successfully.

Locomotion

All the early railways used horses to move the wagons along the rails. Sometimes, as you will see from the picture on page 115, wagons would be allowed to roll down a slope (provided the man sitting on the wagon had a good hand-brake!), and horses would be used to pull them along level ground and up inclines. There were steam engines in use in the mines, but these were all fixed engines. They were used to pump water from the mine workings, or, more rarely, to winch wagons along the rails. No one had yet thought of making the engine move.

An Act of Parliament in 1801 allowed the first public railway – the Surrey Iron Railway – to be built. It ran from Wandsworth in London to Croydon in Surrey. Five years later the Oystermouth Railway, which was the first public passenger service, opened in Swansea, South Wales. By 1825 there were about thirty of these railways in all parts of Britain. They all had one thing in common: horses pulled the wagons and carriages along the rails.

Shortly before his death in 1803, the old Duke of Bridgewater, who had built the first canals, exclaimed

'Canals will last my lifetime, but what I fear is the tramways.'

He had no need to fear, so long as nobody hit upon the idea of combining a fixed iron rail with a moving steam engine.

Richard Trevithick

In 1800 the patent which James Watt held on the steam engines he developed and built ended. This meant that anyone could use, and try to improve upon, his designs. At the same time, the wars with France (1793–1815) meant that the army badly needed horses. This not only meant that good, strong, healthy horses were in short supply, but the price of those that were available was being pushed up. Horse power for tramways and railways was becoming expensive.

A Cornish mining engineer, Richard Trevithick, set to work. In 1802 he patented a high pressure steam engine. This used super-heated steam, and worked at a pressure which was six or seven times greater than the surrounding atmosphere. These new engines could produce more power without having to be built bigger.

James Watt had always refused to work with anything much greater than atmospheric pressure, fearing an explosion. Richard Trevithick showed, however, that by proper use of safety valves, explosions were very unlikely to happen. His engines were well designed and reliable, and Trevithick was kept busy arranging the supply of high-pressure stationary steam engines to a variety of businesses and companies.

Things, however, went badly wrong in 1803 because Trevithick's instructions about the operation of his high-pressure engines had not been followed. One of these engines was being used to pump water from a building site in Greenwich, and Trevithick explained what happened in a letter to his friend, Davies Gilbert:

'It appears the boy that had the care of the engine was gon to catch eales in the foundation of the building, and left the care of it to one of the Labourers; this labourer saw the engine working much faster than usual, stop'd it without taking off a spanner which fastened down the steam lever, and a short time after being Idle it burst. It killed 3 on the spot and one other is seance dead of his wounds . . .

However, this tragedy caused only a temporary setback, and orders for high-pressure steam engines continued to be made by those businesses which needed to use fast, efficient pumps.

It was then that Trevithick hit upon a revolutionary idea. His new steam engine used less fuel than the old ones, and was so much lighter that it could be carried on a cart. Why not, then, use the steam engine to power the cart?

Idea followed idea, and it took all Trevithick's engineering skills to carry them out. Finally, in February 1804, his locomotive pulled five wagons, a coach and seventy passengers from the Pen-y-Daren Ironworks near Merthyr Tydfil in South Wales to the Glamorganshire canal. The distance they travelled was about 10 miles, and the whole journey took about four hours. This was the first steam engine to run on rails and pull a train behind it. The Duke of Bridgewater's nightmare had come true!

Richard Trevithick's railroad at Euston in 1809

Four years later, Richard Trevithick's engine *Catch-Me-Who-Can* was giving shilling rides on a circular track in London at the fantastic speed of twelve miles-per-hour. Unbeknown to Richard Trevithick, the site he had chosen was, thirty years later, to be developed as Euston Station.

However, disaster was to strike, as this letter to the *Mechanics' Magazine*, written in March 1847, explains:

'Sir,
. . . about the year 1808 he [*Richard Trevithick*] laid down a circular railway in a field adjoining the New Road . . . he placed a locomotive engine, weighing about 10 tons, on that railway . . . at the rate of twelve miles an hour . . . Mr Trevithick then gave his opinion that it would go twenty miles an hour, or more, on a straight railway . . . the engine was exhibited at one shilling admittance, including a ride for the few who were not too timid . . . it ran

for some weeks, when a rail broke and occasioned the engine to fly off in a tangent and overturn, the ground being very soft at the time.

Mr Trevithick having expended all his means in erecting the works and enclosure, and shillings not having come in fast enough to pay current expenses, the engine was not again set on the rail.
I am, Sir, your obedient servant,
John Isaac Hawkins
Civil Engineer, London.'

Richard Trevithick did not have the money to develop his steam locomotive any further, nor did he manage to find wealthy people to back him. He died, a poor man, in 1833. Others, however, realised the importance of what he had done in making a steam engine move along rails, pulling a load. They were to take his brilliant idea and develop it far further than maybe he had ever dreamed.

The First Railway Companies: (1) The Stockton to Darlington Railway

Groups of businessmen gradually realised that large profits could be made from railways. They were prepared to put their money into forming railway companies. First, the company would have to get the permission of Parliament to build a railway. Then the job of the company would be to buy land, hire surveyors to plan the line of the railway, hire engineers to build the track and the engines, and, finally, employ drivers, guards and signalmen to work the railway properly and safely. Members of the public would be able to buy shares in a railway company, and would share in that company's profits. They would also, of course, share in any losses too!

Canal or Rail?

For some time, the coal owners and the coal traders in the Darlington area of the north-east of England had wanted a quicker and cheaper way of transporting coal from the coalfields of South Durham to the port of Stockton on the River Tees. Some wanted a canal to be dug direct to Stockton; others wanted a railway which could collect coal from all the collieries before going on to Stockton. Those who argued for a railway won the day, and the Stockton and Darlington Company was set up. A private Act of Parliament gave the Company permission to build a railway. Now all that had to be done was to find an engineer to build it.

Choosing an Engineer

Richard Trevithick, you will remember, had been a mining engineer. The work he had done in actually making a steam engine move, using its own power, had impressed and fascinated many other mining engineers. Several of them developed his ideas further. In 1812 John Blenkinsop had designed a steam engine, *The Prince Regent*, and had begun to operate a steam railway on the outskirts of Leeds. A year later William Hedley had built *Puffing Billy*, a steam engine which could pull nine laden wagons at about five miles-per-hour.

In 1814 George Stephenson (1741–1848), the mining engineer at Killingworth Colliery, had used ideas from Richard Trevithick, John Blenkinsop and William Hedley, and had built the steam engine *Blucher*. His engineering skills were much in demand, and he worked part-time for several collieries in the north-east. Between 1814 and 1821 he designed and built sixteen more locomotives, and laid many miles of track.

The directors of the Stockton and Darlington Company did not seem to have had a very difficult job in deciding whom to ask to work for them. In 1821 the Quaker businessman Edward Pease, on behalf of the Company, invited George Stephenson to work for them as engineer-in-charge. He was given a £600, part-time contract.

Surveying and Track-laying

The line between Stockton and Darlington was carefully surveyed, and the twenty-seven-mile route between Witton Park Colliery, via Darlington, to Stockton, was constructed. It was a single-line track, with loops to let trains pass each other. Wrought iron rails were laid at a distance of 4 feet 8½ inches apart. This particular distance was worked out by George Stephenson, who measured the distance between the wheels on over 100 carts, and calculated the average. This gauge (about 1.5 metres) is still used today.

Horse-power or Steam-power?

How would the wagons move along the rails? It was by no means certain that steam locomotives would be

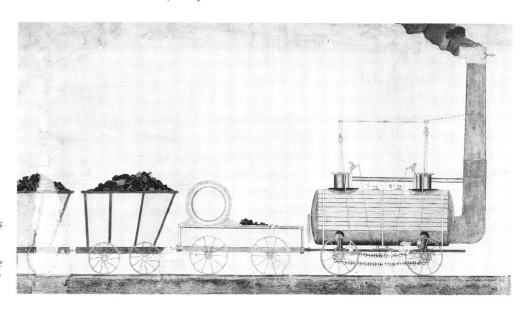

George Stephenson's own drawing of his locomotive, built in 1814, for use on the Killingworth colliery wagonway

A contemporary sketch of the opening of the Stockton to Darlington Railway, 1825

used. Indeed, Edward Pease had assumed that George Stephenson would prefer to use horses. However, George Stephenson and his son Robert (1803–59) had other ideas. When the Stockton to Darlington line was opened in September 1825, it was the steam engine *Locomotion* which pulled wagons for passengers and for coals along iron rails lined by cheering crowds. George Stephenson himself had not, however, planned to use steam locomotives for the whole of the twenty-seven miles of track between Stockton and Darlington. At the Witton Park Colliery end of the line he had built winding engines on the top of two hills. The track in-between them was for horses only. The rest of the track could be used either by horses or by steam locomotives.

Robert Stephenson worked with his father on many projects. It is sometimes difficult for historians to disentangle exactly which one of them did what. However, it does seem clear that *Locomotion* was designed by George Stephenson and built by Robert Stephenson in his own engine works.

Opening the Railway

In the picture above you can see the cheering crowds, and *Locomotion* steaming along the track. The whole train was made up of the engine itself, the tender, with coal and water; six wagons laden with coal and flour, a covered coach in which travelled the owners and members of the railway committee; twenty-one wagons carrying passengers and, finally, six laden with coal. The whole train moved at speeds of between twelve and fifteen miles-per-hour. Fields surrounding the track were filled with cheering people. The celebrations con-

tinued afterwards, as the *Local Records of Northumberland and Durham* show:

> 'The engine, with its load, arrived in Darlington, a distance of $8\frac{3}{4}$ miles in 65 minutes . . . By the time the cavalcade arrived at Stockton, where it was received with great joy, there were not less than 600 persons within, and hanging by the carriages. Part of the workmen were entertained at Stockton and part at Yarm; and there was a grand dinner for the proprietors and their most distinguished guests, to the number of 102, at the Town-hall in Stockton . . .'

Success

J. Francis, in his book *A History of the English Railway*, which was published in 1851, was certain that the Stockton to Darlington railway was a great success. This is part of what he says:

> 'In addition to the social advantages which accrued from increased communication – and who shall doubt the fireside union, the social pleasure, and the domestic happiness it conferred? – was the development of commerce, and the increased importance of the various places through which it passed. A new trade in lime arose; the carriage in lead was enormously reduced in cost; the price of coal fell from 18s to 8s 6d; the landowners received large sums for gravel, timber, and stone, taken from their estates. An obscure fishing village was changed into a considerable seaport town. The Stockton and Darlington railway turned the

shop-keeper into a merchant, erected an exchange; gave bread to hundreds; and conferred happiness on thousands. . .'

This was written in 1851, when railways were well established in most parts of Britain. But in 1825, when the Stockton–Darlington railway was opened, it was by no means certain that any more railways with steam-powered locomotives would be built anywhere else in the country. The Stockton–Darlington railway itself had horse-drawn wagons running along part of its length for several years. Indeed, it was by no means certain that steam-power would ever completely replace horse-power on the railways.

The First Railway Companies: (2) The Liverpool to Manchester Railway

The Cost of Canals

A number of Liverpool merchants were becoming more and more unhappy at the high charges they had to pay for using local canals and waterways. They were determined to break the power of the canal companies, and find a cheaper and better way of moving goods such as cotton and sugar between the port of Liverpool and the city of Manchester. They formed a company to build a railway between the two cities.

Problems in Parliament

The Liverpool and Manchester Railway Company's first attempt to get an Act of Parliament allowing them to build a railway failed in 1825. The Stockton–Darlington line had been built instead of a canal; the proposed Liverpool–Manchester line was to replace a canal. If the line was successful, the canal companies and the canal trade would fail. Owners of canal companies, and landowners with shares in canal companies, combined to try to defeat the Liverpool to Manchester railway before it had even begun.

The following year, however, the Company was successful. An Act of Parliament allowed them to build a double track, about thirty-three miles long, between Manchester and Liverpool. The Company engaged George Stephenson as their chief engineer, and paid him £1,000 per year.

Problems of construction

The Company's troubles, however, were not over. The landowners continued their opposition to the plan, and surveyors frequently had to flee for their lives; George Stephenson remembered one occasion:

'I was threatened to be ducked in the pond if I proceeded, and, of course, we had a great deal of

the survey to take by stealth, at the time when the people were at dinner. We could not get it done by night; indeed we were watched by day and night, and guns were discharged over the grounds belonging to Captain Bradshaw to prevent us.'

There were natural obstacles, too. It was here that all George Stephenson's skill and ingenuity were needed. The vast peaty bog of Chat Moss had to be crossed somehow, though there were those who doubted whether it could ever be done. Giving evidence to the parliamentary committee, George Stephenson described the problem:

'In the centre, where this railroad is to cross, it is all pulp from the top to the depth of 34 feet; at 34 feet there is a vein of 4 or 6 inches of clay; below that there are 2 or 3 feet of quicksand; and the bottom of that is hard clay, which keeps all the water in . . .'

Hundreds of tons of earth and rubble were sunk into Chat Moss; when a solid surface appeared through the mud and slime, brushwood rafts were floated on top on which the track could be laid.

A second obstacle was the Sankey Brook Navigation, which the railway had to cross. George Stephenson designed a special viaduct for this, which carried the track high above the waterway. Near Liverpool a tunnel almost a mile-and-a-quarter long had to be bored through solid rock, and a cutting called the Olive Mount Cutting, 100 feet deep had to be made. These were necessary because it was important that the track was laid on ground which was as flat and level as possible.

Surveying the land and laying the track went ahead before the decision had been made as to what, exactly, was to pull the wagons. George and Robert Stephenson wanted steam locomotives to work the whole line, except for the last steep incline near Liverpool. On this part of the track they recommended that stationary steam engines should be used to haul the wagons and carriages up the last stretch. Some of the directors of the Liverpool and Manchester Railway disagreed. They wanted stationary steam engines to haul the trains by rope along the whole length of the track, from Manchester to Liverpool, section by section.

The Rainhill Trials

In order to settle the question, the directors decided to hold a competition on part of the new track at Rainhill, outside Liverpool. A prize of £500 was offered for the best steam engine to work the track. It had to weigh not more than six tons, have no more than six wheels, and had to haul at least twenty tons at no less than ten miles-per-hour.

The Stephensons designed and built a new engine called *Rocket*. It had a revolutionary boiler, which produced a great deal more steam than conventional boilers. More steam, of course, meant greater power. Spies from other engineering works tried desperately to discover what the Stephensons were up to. They

The Rocket *wins the Rainhill trials*

found out on the day of the competition in October 1829!

Six engines took part in the competition, and each engine was allowed to make twenty runs on the 2 miles of track. Each time, the judges checked each engine for speed, the amount of water and fuel used, and any time spent having repairs done. The *Rocket* emerged a clear winner. The engine did not fail on even one of her runs, and on the final one managed a top speed of twenty-nine miles-per-hour. All her competitors either exploded or broke down at least once!

The directors' minds were made up. Steam locomotives were to be used on the whole length of the Liverpool–Manchester railway, except for the last steep incline up to Liverpool.

Triumph and Disaster

The railway connecting the city of Manchester and the port of Liverpool was officially opened on 15th September 1830, amid great rejoicing. The Prime Minister, the Duke of Wellington, was present, together with Sir Robert Peel (who was to become Prime Minister later in the century) and William Huskisson, the MP for Liverpool, who had done so much to support the original proposals for a railway when they were discussed by the House of Commons. Amid cheering crowds the guests were taken on a special excursion. It was then that disaster struck. The engine stopped to take on more water, and some of the important guests got down to watch what was happening and generally

look around. William Huskisson, totally unused to tracks and steam locomotives, was knocked down by an engine travelling in the opposite direction. His leg was smashed, and an amputation seemed the only way to save his life. The engine was unhooked from the wagons and carriages it was pulling, and took William Huskisson to Manchester at the unheard of speed of thirty-two miles-per-hour. In spite of all the efforts of the doctors, he died the following day.

Success

The railway was an almost instant success. Within a month of opening it was carrying over 1,200 passengers a day, 500 more than the stage-coaches could carry. Not only did the railway carry more people, but it carried them at over twice the speed and for half the cost. By the end of the first year, freight was being carried as well as passengers. Part of the route of the new railway went through the village of Newton. Newton had two Members of Parliament. The vast city of Manchester, with over 180,000 inhabitants, was not represented in Parliament at all.

Merchants, industrialists and businessmen were well pleased with the venture. So, too, were those hundreds of people who had risked their money to buy shares in the Liverpool to Manchester Railway Company. They were making excellent profits – profits which would encourage many more to back this new system of travel.

SOURCE WORK:
The First Railways

1. Look back at pages 116–7.
   Richard Trevithick was the first engineer to realise that the power produced by steam engines could be used to move the engines themselves. In 1804 he made a steam locomotive which pulled five wagons, a coach and seventy passengers for ten miles along a track in Wales. In 1808 *Catch-Me-Who-Can* gave rides around a circular track in London.
   Why, then, did a passenger-carrying rail network not begin to develop at that time?

SOURCE A

This is part of a letter written by George Stephenson to Edward Pease in 1824. Lord Derby, Lord Sefton and Captain Bradshaw owned shares in the Bridgewater Canal, and land on the route of the proposed Liverpool–Manchester railway.

'We have had sad work with Lord Derby, Lord Sefton and Bradshaw the great Canal Proprietor whose ground we go through with the projected railway. Their ground is blockaded on every side to prevent us getting on with the survey. Bradshaw fires guns through his grounds in the course of the night to prevent the surveyors coming in the dark. We are to have a grand field day next week. The Liverpool Rly Co. are determined to force a survey through if possible. Lord Sefton says he will have 100 men to stop us. The Company thinks those great men have no right to stop our survey.'

(Quoted in L.T.C. Rolt, *George and Robert Stephenson*, Longman, 1957)

2. Read Source A. Now read again the first extract on page 120.
   (a) How might Lord Sefton and Captain Bradshaw have explained the way in which they were behaving?
   (b) How might George Stephenson have explained his determination to get the survey carried out?
   (c) Why didn't Lord Derby, Lord Sefton and Captain Bradshaw solve their problems by selling their shares in canal companies, and buying shares in the new railway companies?

SOURCE B

The *Annual Register*, which was published every year, contained a review of all the main events of the past year. In 1832 it described the changes which the railway was bringing:

'All the coaches but one have ceased running . . . the canals have reduced their rates 30 per cent. Goods are delivered in Manchester the same day as they are received in Liverpool. By canal they were never delivered before the third day . . . the saving to manufacturers in the neighbourhood of Manchester, in the carriage of cotton alone, has been £20,000 per annum . . . Coal pits have been sunk, and manufactories established on the line, giving great employment to the poor . . . The railway pays one fifth of the poor-rates in the parishes through which it passes . . . It is found advantageous for the carriage of milk and garden produce . . . Residents on the line find the railway a great convenience by enabling them to attend to their business in Manchester and Liverpool with ease, at little expense. No inconvenience is felt by residents from smoke or noise . . . The value of land on the line has been considerably enhanced by the operation of the railway; land cannot be purchased but at a large increase in price. It is much sought after for building . . . much waste land on the line has been taken into cultivation, and yields a good rent.'

(From *Annual Register*, 1832, Miscellaneous Articles)

3. Explain carefully whether or not, according to Source B, the following people would have benefited from the Liverpool–Manchester railway:
   (i) the owner of a Manchester cotton mill;
   (ii) a farmer who wanted to sell fresh vegetables;
   (iii) a landowner who had a large number of canal company shares;
   (iv) a pauper;
   (v) a stage-coach driver;
   (vi) a businessman living ten miles outside Liverpool.

4. Read pages 115–21 again.
   Richard Trevithick was the first engineer to prove that steam engines could power themselves to move along a fixed track.
   George Stephenson was the first engineer to design a public, steam-powered passenger carrying service. Which of the two men was the more important in the development of railways?

The First Railways

SOURCE C

STEAMED OUT,

or the Starving Stage-Coachman and Boys.

5. Cartoons are not always funny.
   (a) What serious point was George Cruikshank trying to make when he drew this cartoon?
   (b) Cartoons and pictures usually tell us a great deal about the period in which they were drawn or painted. What can you find out from this cartoon?

6. Everything listed below contributed in some way to the building of the Stockton-Darlington and the Manchester-Liverpool railways:
   (i) the use of wooden railways in coal-mining areas;
   (ii) Richard Reynold's invention of the flanged rail;
   (iii) the development of wrought iron;
   (iv) Richard Trevithick's engine *Catch-Me-Who-Can*.
   (v) the need for industrialists to move manufactured goods and raw materials more quickly than the canals could carry them;
   (a) How did *each* contribute to the development of the first steam railways?
   (b) Which was the most important?
   (c) Is any one of these *less* important than any of the others?
   Use the sources and information on pages 115–21 to help you explain your answers.

Track, Track and More Track

Date	Miles of track open	Passengers carried	Money from passengers	Money from freight
1825	27			
1830	98			
1834	298			
1838	743	5.4 m		
1842	1,939			
1846	3,036	40.2 m	£4.6 m	£2.8 m
1850	6,084	67.4 m	£6.5 m	£6.2 m
1852	6,628	82.8 m	£7.3 m	£7.7 m

This table shows just how quickly track was being laid down

Railway Companies

No one planned this new transport system. Companies, like the Stockton to Darlington Railway Company and the Manchester to Liverpool Railway Company, were set up wherever a group of businessmen or speculators thought there was profit to be made. Cities and ports were linked by railway lines, as were business centres and industrial cities. Sometimes more than one company would build a rail link between the same two towns. Investors then had to choose the company they thought would bring in the most profit. The people who used the line had to choose the one which gave them the best service. Sometimes both lines would prosper; sometimes one – or both – would fail. The important thing to remember is that lines were only built where people thought they would make money.

By 1851 five companies owned about half of all the track which had been laid down in Britain. These companies were the Great Northern, the Great Western, the Midland, the London and North-Western, and the York and North Midland. The remaining lines were owned by hundreds of small companies. Clearly it became very difficult for people (or goods) to make a long journey which crossed company boundaries: separate bookings had to be made with each railway company, and each company charged different rates and operated different timetables.

Railway Mania

Between 1844 and 1848 a 'railway madness' gripped the country. Parliament considered 909 proposals for new lines, and agreed to 12,000 miles of track being built. It was never really likely that all that track would actually be built. Furthermore, it was even less likely that all the track which was built would make a profit. That, however, did not stop the speculators. Everyone who could afford it rushed to buy railway shares, no matter whether the proposed lines were sensible and likely to make a reasonable profit, or not.

J. Francis, in his book *A History of the English Railway* which was published in 1851, described the 'mania':

'. . . Three distinct lines were proposed to Norwich. Surrey was entirely mapped and marked out . . . in one parish of a metropolitan borough, sixteen schemes were afloat, and upwards of one thousand two hundred houses scheduled to be taken down . . . in Durham three railroads had been attempted . . . all running in parallel lines . . . The wildest schemes were calmly entertained . . . One . . . proposed sails to propel his engine, and induced a company to try them. Another offered to propel his locomotives with rockets, confidently promising 100 miles [*160 km*] an hour . . .'

Something had to happen. The mania could not continue for ever.

George Hudson, the Railway King

The man who did much to create – and end – the railway mania was George Hudson. At the beginning of the railway boom he was a draper in York. The turning-point in his life came when he was left £30,000. He used the money to buy shares in a new line which was being built to join York to the Leeds–Derby line. George Hudson's aim was to make York the centre of a railway network – a network which he, of course, would control. He very nearly managed it.

He became Chairman of the York and Midland Railway, and he financed the building of the King's Cross to Edinburgh line. By buying up smaller companies, he managed to control over 1,600 km of railway lines. The newspapers began to call him the 'Railway King'. The magazine *Punch* printed a cartoon (opposite) showing George Hudson on a mock throne with all kinds of people, rich and poor, bowing down in front of him.

He was admired and respected by many. He was twice made Mayor of York, and became MP for Sunderland in 1845. However, George Stephenson gave a warning:

'I have made Hudson a rich man, but he will very soon care for nobody except he can get money from them.'

The bubble was soon to burst. George Hudson had too much money tied up in too many schemes. Some

KING HUDSON'S LEVEE.

of his lines were making a loss. However, the shareholders never guessed. They received their regular payments as usual. George Hudson was paying them by using money given to him by other shareholders to invest in other lines. This clearly could not go on for very long. It was also illegal. George Hudson was found out. His companies collapsed in 1849, and he was sent to prison for debt.

George Hudson's fate was a dreadful shock to many people. They began to look seriously at their own investments. They took money out of schemes which looked doubtful, and put it in those railways which looked as though they were likely to make a good profit. Railway mania was over.

The Parliamentary Train

Most railway companies had three different kinds of carriage – and three different prices for tickets. First-class carriages were used by the really wealthy people; second-class carriages by businessmen and middle-class industrialists and shopkeepers; and third-class carriages by the working classes who could not afford to pay for anything better. Many trains did not have a third class, and some companies only ran third-class carriages at night.

Parliament, as you have seen, was never very keen to interfere in what it believed to be the private affairs of companies, businesses and individuals. However, in this case it did. The Railway Act was passed in 1844. It stated that at least one train per day (except Christmas Day and Good Friday) was to travel the whole length of every line, to and from the terminus, stopping at every station. Seats were to be provided, and the passengers were to be protected from the weather. No railway company could charge more than one penny for each mile travelled, and the trains had to travel at a minimum speed of twelve miles-per-hour. This meant that most working-class people could now afford to make the journeys which they wanted to make: whether it was one or two stations to work, or, perhaps, the whole length of the line for a special visit.

The Battle of the Gauges

George and Robert Stephenson, as you have seen, built their railway track with a gap of 4 feet $8\frac{1}{2}$ inches between each rail. This distance between the rails is called the gauge. The Great Western Railway, however, was built by Isambard Kingdom Brunel (1806–59), who had other ideas. He worked out carefully the exact gauge needed to allow wagons and carriages to travel smoothly and at speed – and came up with a gauge of 7 feet $\frac{1}{2}$ inch. As Brunel was the Chief Engineer for the Great Western Railway Company, all the track laid down by that Company was built to the broad gauge, and not to Stephenson's narrower gauge. All would have been well, provided that companies, industries, businessmen and ordinary people wanted to travel on track owned by one company only. Of course they did not. Many journeys made by people, and many journeys booked by firms and companies wanting to shift raw materials or finished goods, were made on the track of more than one company. This meant that people had to change trains when the track gauge changed, and goods had to be shifted to different sized wagons. This clearly took a great deal of time and caused a great deal of confusion. There was not just one place in the system where the gauge changed; there were about thirty 'break of gauge' points.

Some track had a third rail, and would take either broad-gauge or narrower-gauge wagons and carriages, but this was expensive to build and so there was not very much of it.

Brunel suggested that the whole matter could be sorted out by holding speed trials. In mid-December 1845 the steam engine *Ixion* made three round trips between Paddington and Exeter with loads of 60, 70 and 80 tons. The *Ixion's* speed touched sixty miles-per-hour with the maximum load, and averaged out at fifty miles-per-hour with a load of 60 tons. This was far faster than any of her rivals from the other companies. The fastest could only make a speed of fifty-three miles-per-hour with a 50-ton load, while the *Stephenson* ran off the rails and turned over!

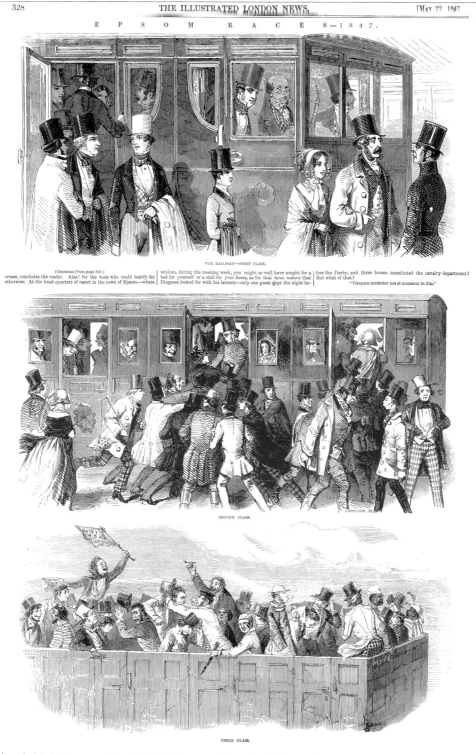

328   THE ILLUSTRATED LONDON NEWS.   [MAY 22, 1847.

E P S O M   R A C E S — 1 8 4 7.

THE RAILWAY—FIRST CLASS.

(Continued from page 325.)

crease, concludes the reader. Alas! for the *hosts* who could testify far otherwise. At the head-quarters of resort in the town of Epsom—where

whilom, during the meeting week, you might as well have sought for a bed for yourself or a stall for your horse, as for that *lucus naturæ* that Diogenes looked for with his lantern—only one guest slept the night be-

fore the Derby, and three horses constituted the cavalry department! But what of that?

"*Tempora mutantur nos et mutamur in illis.*"

SECOND CLASS.

HARRISON. Sc.

THIRD CLASS.

First, second and third class as printed in the Illustrated London News, *1847*

The judges were not, however, convinced. The broad gauge was clearly safer, the carriages were more comfortable, and it allowed journeys to be made more quickly. However, cost played an important part in their decision. Not only was it cheaper to narrow a gauge than to widen it, but only 274 miles of broad-gauge track were in operation, compared with the 1,900 miles of the narrower kind. Parliament therefore decided that the narrower gauge of the Stephensons was to become standard throughout Britain. Companies which used the broad gauge were given until the 1890s to alter it and build new rolling stock.

Brunel may have lost the 'Battle of the Gauges', but the battle itself certainly encouraged engineers to develop steam-engine design and increase steam engine performance.

SOURCE WORK:
Travelling by Train

SOURCE A

In March 1825 the *Quarterly Review*, which was a Tory journal, contained an article which was about travelling by train. This is part of what it said:

'What can be more ridiculous than the idea of trains travelling twice as fast as stage coaches! We should as soon expect people to let themselves be fired off upon a rocket as to trust themselves to the mercy of such a machine going at such a speed.'

(From *Quarterly Review*, March 1825)

SOURCE B

A passenger on one of the early railways described a journey he made:

'I started at five o'clock on Sunday evening, got to Birmingham by half-past five on Monday morning [*by coach*] and got upon the rail-road by half-past seven. Nothing can be more comfortable than the vehicle in which I was put . . . and there is nothing disagreeable about it but the occasional whiffs of stinking air which is impossible to exclude altogether. The first sensation is a slight degree of nervousness and a feeling of being run away with, but a sense of security soon supervenes [*takes its place*], and the velocity [*speed*] is delightful. Town after town, one park and chateau after another are left behind with the rapid variety of a moving panorama, and the constant bustle . . . of the changes and stoppages made the journey very entertaining.'

(From *Greville Memoirs*, 18 July 1837)

1. Read Sources A and B.
   Source A was written in 1825. Source B was written in 1837.
   How was it possible for such different ideas about rail travel to be held within such a short space of time?

SOURCE C

F. Coghlan wrote a book in 1838 called *The Iron Road*. Part of the book gave advice to travellers in third-class open wagons:

'Get as far from the engine as possible for three reasons. First, should an explosion take place you may happily get off with the loss of an arm or a leg. Secondly, the vibration is very much diminished the further you get from the engine. Thirdly, always sit with your back towards the engine, by this plan you will avoid being chilled by a cold current of air which passes through these open waggons, and also save you from being blinded by the small cinders which escape from the funnel.'

(From F. Coghlan, *The Iron Road*, 1838)

SOURCE D

A passenger remembered a problem which happened on long journeys:

'Fortunately after many hours the train stopped long enough at a small station in northern England for the men to take to the woods and the females to make for the ladies' waiting room where a long queue formed outside the single WC. The maids – low in the pecking order, as it were, – had to use the coal skuttle.'

(Quoted in I. Smullen, *Taken for a Ride*, 1968)

2. Read Sources C and D.
   (a) What evidence is there in Sources C and D that travelling by rail did have problems for the passengers?
   (b) Use your own knowledge of the state of railways to explain whether or not these were the only problems which faced rail travellers at this time.
   (c) If travelling by rail was so full of problems, why did people travel by train at all?

The Railway Navvies

Building railways was becoming big business. Railway companies employed engineers like George and Robert Stephenson, and Isambard Kingdom Brunel, to plan lines and design locomotives, bridges and viaducts. They would not, however, allow one person to be in charge of actually building the whole line: it was far too big a job. The London–Birmingham line, for example, was built in sections, and each section was the responsibility of a different contractor. This contractor was responsible for everything to do with laying his particular section of track. He had to hire and pay the men who did the manual work, provide all the material needed, and complete the job by an agreed date. When a line was about to be built, contractors put in tenders (said how much they would charge the railway company) for building sections of track, or for building bridges, viaducts and tunnels. These were usually contracted separately. The railway companies did not always accept the lowest tender. A lot depended on what they thought of the contractor and whether they believed he would finish the job satisfactorily and on time.

A navvy with his gear

King of the Labourers

The actual hard grind of moving thousands of tons of earth and boulders, of blasting tunnels through solid rock, of lining dripping tunnels with clay bricks, was not done by the engineers or by the contractors. It was not done by machines. It was done by the 'navvies', who risked their lives every day to build just one more mile of track.

Navvies (named after the 'navigators' who dug the canals) were more than just labourers. Navvies were the specialists. It was they who blasted tunnels through solid rock, who built the huge viaducts which carried railway track above rivers, canals, valleys and cities, and provided the skilled labour to dig cuttings like the one at Tring on the London–Birmingham line. This cut-

The Tring cutting painted by J.C Bourne in 1837. You can see how each gang of navvies worked separately, and yet were all working together to make the cutting

ting was forty feet deep and ran for three miles through solid chalk.

Local labourers, from the villages and towns through which the railway was passing, filled the wagons with earth and debris and carted it away. They would work on the railway for as long as it was close to where they lived. When it moved too far on, they would look for other work. Navvies, however, worked together until a particular project was finished. They moved along the line together in tight-knit groups. Even their clothes were different from those of ordinary labourers. Navvies, according to Terry Coleman who wrote a book about them in 1965, wore:

> '. . . moleskin trousers, double-canvas shirts, velveteen square tailed coats, hobnail boots, gaudy handkerchiefs, and white felt hats with the brims turned up.'

Between jobs on the railways, navvies would work on other projects. Thomas Brassey, a wealthy and successful contractor, took a group of them to the Crimea. There, during the war between Russia, France and Great Britain, they built railways and survived the Russian winter better than most of the soldiers. Other navvies worked on docks and roads. One gang was responsible for building the Crystal Palace, about which you will read in the next chapter.

Death and Disaster

The life of a navvy was often short because the work which they did was extremely dangerous. They had to clear tonnes of earth and rocks. The most usual way to do this was by 'undermining'. Gangs would burrow away, undermining great banks of soil and sheer rock. Once the navvies had gone in far enough, the overhanging mass of mud and rocks would collapse of its own accord. Too often the navvies, in a hurry to complete the work, would tunnel too far. Hundreds of men were buried alive in such accidents, taking risks in order to build the railways quickly.

A working shaft in the Kilsby Tunnel painted by J.C Bourne in 1837. Bourne made a series of paintings during the construction of the London to Birmingham line. The picture of Tring cutting on page 128 is another in this series

Sometimes the contractors were not careful enough. The Woodhead tunnel runs for three miles underneath the wild moorland and barren rocks of the Pennines between Sheffield and Manchester. Thirty-two navvies died building it. A Manchester surgeon, John Roberton about whom you read on pages 41 and 64, reported in 1845 that, as well as the dead, there were twenty-three cases of compound fractures, seventy-four cases of simple fractures, and another 140 serious cases, including burns from blasts, cuts and dislocations. These deaths and accidents were so serious, and the living conditions of the men and their families were so bad, that Parliament held an enquiry. Here it became quite clear that some contractors did not care how many navvies died, provided the tunnel was built. Wellington Purdon, the assistant engineer, was asked why he did not use safety fuses when blasting. He replied:

'. . . it [*the use of safety fuses*] is attended with such a loss of time . . . I would not recommend the loss of time for the sake of all the extra lives it would save.'

Sometimes death was the navvies' own fault. Three were killed playing a wild game of follow-my-leader, which involved jumping across the huge navigation shafts built for the Kilsby tunnel on the London–Birmingham line.

Engineers and contractors did not find this number of deaths and accidents at all surprising, or even alarming. Brunel, when shown the casualty list (made between September 1839 and June 1841) of the 131 navvies hurt or killed whilst building the Great Western Railway, said that he thought the number was really very small:

'. . . considering the very heavy works and the immense amount of powder used, and some of the heaviest and most difficult works; I am afraid it does not show the whole extent of accidents incurred. . .'

Living Conditions

Navvies had to live on the job. John Francis, who wrote *A History of the English Railway* published in 1851, described their living conditions:

'. . . They made their homes where they got their work. Some slept in huts constructed of damp turf, cut from wet grass, too low to stand upright in . . . Others formed a room of stones without mortar, placed thatch . . . across the roof, and took possession of it with their families, often making a source of profit by lodging as many of their fellow-workmen as they could crowd in. It matters not to them that the rain beat through the roof, and that the wind swept through the holes . . .'

Large numbers of men, crowded together for months on end, created other problems. John Francis goes on to say that:

'In such places from nine to fifteen hundred men were crowded . . . Living like brutes, they were depraved, degraded and reckless. Drunkenness and dissoluteness of morals prevailed. There were many women, but few wives . . .'

Indeed, in some navvy communities, a sort of wedding ceremony took place. A navvy and his woman would jump over a broom handle together – this was enough.

Navvies were physically very strong. Many, however, died or were terribly injured in accidents whilst building the line. Almost as many died from disease and illness. John Roberton, a Manchester surgeon, visited the navvies' encampments while they were building the Woodhead tunnel. So did Henry Pomfret, a surgeon from Hollingworth, who was paid by the navvies to visit the tunnel three days a week to treat men's injuries. Their notes and journals provide evidence of sickness and disease as well as injuries among the navvies.

'. . . Many had chronic coughs, which they blamed on the moistness of the tunnel. Their clothes became soaked before they had been at work a quarter of an hour. Roberton asked a woman in one of the huts how ten or fourteen lodgers in one hut could dry all their wet clothes by a single fire. She answered that the clothes were seldom half dry. Pomfret said the coughs were caused by this perpetual dampness and also by the inhaling of dense gunpowder smoke with which the tunnel was commonly filled.'

Tickets and Tommy-shops

Contractors, of course, had to pay the navvies. But they did not always pay them money. Many contractors 'paid' the navvies tickets which were worth a certain amount of money. The navvies could exchange these tickets at a tommy-shop for ale and spirits, bread, meat, bacon, tobacco, shovels, jackets, boots and many other goods. At the end of a month, the navvy's pay was calculated, and the amount he had 'spent' in tickets was taken away from the total. The balance was paid in cash. However, most tommy-shops were owned, or partly owned, by the contractors. The contractors could charge high prices and make a profit from the navvies they were employing. There was a great deal of cheating by both navvies and contractors.

Most contractors employed navvies. There were two great contractors, who between them built most of the track in Great Britain: Thomas Brassey (1805–70) and Samuel Morton Peto (1809–89). Peto, like Thomas Brassey, was well respected by those he employed; like Brassey he took on a lot of work overseas, and he, too, amassed a large fortune before he died. In 1855 Peto was made a baronet for building an army railway in the Crimea, and for being one of the commissioners of the 1851 Great Exhibition. Perhaps Samuel Peto should have the last word on navvies:

'. . . if you pay him well, and show you care for him, he is the most faithful and hardworking creature in existence; . . . He will be your faithful servant . . .'

He 'will be home today . . .'

In 1859 a book called *The Triumph of Steam* was published which, among other things, described the benefits of the railways:

> 'Only fancy, Aunt Helen, that Uncle Henry was in Paris yesterday and will be home today. Is it not wonderful? What did men do before there were railroads. . .?'

It was not only Uncle Henry whose life was altered by the railways. The coming of the railways meant that the lives of nearly every man, woman and child were changed – and changed for ever.

Railways and Industry

Railways used thousands of tonnes of coal to fire the steam engines, iron to forge the rails and steel plates to build the locomotives; engineering bricks were needed to line the tunnels, and pumps to drain the workings; picks, shovels, and barrows were needed to move the earth from cuttings and to build embankments. Stations and signal boxes had to be built, and so did engine sheds and engineering works. This great demand for such things as coal, iron and steel, machine-tools and bricks, meant that the industries which produced them had to expand, and in doing so

take on hundreds more workers. Industrial output soared. There were new jobs, too, on the railways. People were employed as engine drivers and signalmen, as station masters, porters and cleaners.

New towns were built because of the railways. The Great Western Railway built a great locomotive works at a point half-way between London and Bristol. This completely changed the small market town of Swindon, which was where the works were built. The picture below, drawn in 1849, shows clearly how the workers' houses (on the right) were separated from the workshops (on the left) by the railway lines.

The tiny hamlet of Crewe was changed for ever by the railways. The railway companies decided to make it a junction for lines linking the midlands, north-west England and Scotland. Engine sheds, locomotive works, shops, churches and workers' houses were all built by the railway companies. In 1841 only 201 people lived there; by 1901 it had a population of 42,074.

Existing towns were greatly enlarged because of the railways. Southampton and Liverpool became important passenger and cargo ports; Dover became a ferry terminal, while fishing ports like Grimsby and Fleetwood enlarged their fishing fleets to meet the demand for fresh fish, and these towns grew in size as a result. Seaside towns like Scarborough and Brighton grew from being resorts which were only visited by the wealthy to being towns which had to cater for rich and poor alike. Expensive hotels for the rich remained, but

A view of New Swindon in 1849

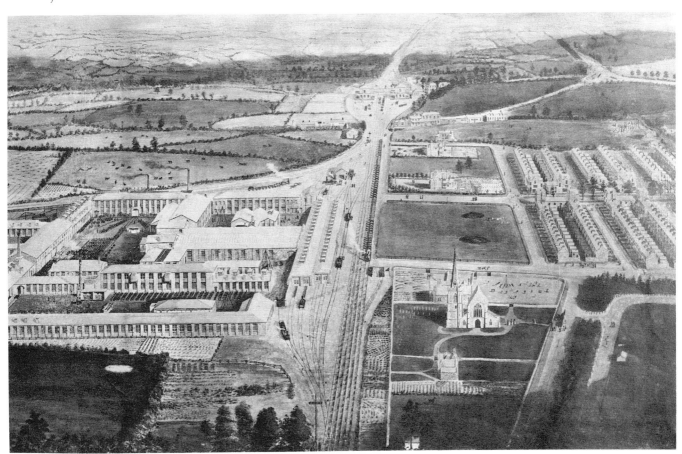

boarding houses and cheap eating places sprung up to cater for the poor.

The railways made a great deal of difference to the way towns looked. Some towns and cities had stations in the very centre, even though this had meant pulling down older buildings. Sometimes it had been impossible to buy land in the very centre of a city, for example in Cambridge, and the station was built almost on the outskirts.

Factories, which were once built near rivers (look back at page 66 to remind yourself why this was) were now built close to railway lines. The coal which they needed to fire furnaces and engines was brought by rail. The goods which were made in the factories and workshops were transported to buyers, markets and ports by rail.

Not everyone benefited. The canals were already losing trade, and the railways ended what was, for many of them, an already shaky existence. The London–Birmingham railway was opened in 1839. By 1844 the Grand Junction Canal, which covered more or less the same route, had lost over half of its freight traffic to the railway. Some canals, however, continued to make a profit until the end of the century.

It was different for the long-distance coaches. Look back at the cartoon on page 123 and at the painting (Source A) on page 134. The building of a rail-link meant the almost instant death of the existing stage-coach and mail-coach services. In 1829, for example, twenty-nine stage-coaches operated each day between Manchester and Liverpool. The Liverpool–Manchester railway opened in 1830. Two years later, only two stage-coaches a day were still in operation. Turnpike roads fell into disuse because the Turnpike Trusts could not raise enough money from the turnpike fees to keep them in good repair. Coaching inns went bankrupt, and many jobs were lost. Some turnpike keepers, stage-coach drivers and inn keepers went to work on the railways; others struggled on, making what living they could. Many became destitute.

Fresh Fish and Seaside Holidays

Railways meant, as you have seen, that communication between towns, cities, villages and ports was much quicker and cheaper than it had been before. This affected not only people, but goods and services as well.

Men, women and children no longer had to stay in their own town or village for most of their lives – or undertake expensive and difficult journeys to get away. They could use the railway to visit friends and relatives elsewhere in the country. They could get to the seaside. All the railway companies with routes to the coast laid on special excursion trains. The cheap rates which were charged meant that poor families could often afford to take these day trips – or stay away for even longer. Many people saw the sea for the first time.

People did not only travel for pleasure. The railways meant that the Chartists could travel between northern towns, and between London and Birmingham, to attend their great rallies (look back at pages 28–32). It

Posters like this advertised the trips and excursions which were now available to many

meant that Chartist speakers could move about easily, and address several rallies in a few days. It also meant, of course, that the government could move troops around quickly to put down any disturbances.

The railways did not only carry people. Fresh meat, fruit, eggs and butter were once only sold locally. The time taken to transport perishable goods to markets further away would have meant that they would have gone rotten on the journey. Now they could be taken to all the main towns in Britain. Fish from Grimsby and Fleetwood, for example, could now be sold in inland towns and cities like Birmingham and Leicester. Many people ate fresh fish for the first time in their lives. The larger towns built markets close to the stations, so that the fish, meat, fruit and vegetables which came in on the overnight train could be sold straight away to local tradesmen. The railways meant that most people had the possibility of a more varied, interesting and healthy diet than before.

Newspapers, letters, parcels and packages were carried by train. The news which was being read at middle-class London breakfast-tables was being read at similar breakfast-tables in Newcastle on the same morning. In 1830 the first mail was carried on the Liverpool–Manchester line, and the Great Western Railway began carrying mail on a regular basis nine years

'Rail over London' by Gustav Doré. Doré (1832–83) was a French engraver, illustrator, painter and sculptor. He is famous for his book illustrations many of which show strange fantasies. He visited London and produced many pictures of the scenes which he saw

later. The new Penny Post, which was introduced in 1840, used the railways. This meant that not only could businesses operate more efficiently by using the railways to carry all their mail, but more people could afford to keep in touch with friends and relations by letter.

As they approached busy main-line stations, railway lines usually passed through those areas where the poor lived. For the first time, the rich and well-to-do could see for themselves the slums and tenements in which the poor, whom they employed, lived.

SOURCE WORK:
The Importance of Railways

SOURCE A

1. Look at Source A.
   (a) What does this picture show?
   (b) What point was the artist trying to make?
   (c) Explain, using your knowledge of the development of railways, whether there is any evidence to support this point.

SOURCE B

The *Railway News* was a magazine which contained items of interest to all those people who were concerned with the railways. The author of this article describes the scene at a busy London terminus in 1864. This scene would not have been possible if it had not been for all the railway construction which had gone on in earlier years.

'In the grey mists of the morning, in the atmosphere of a hundred conflicting smells, and by the light of faintly burning gas, we see a large portion of the supply of the great London markets rapidly disgorged [*unloaded*] by these night trains: fish, flesh and food, Aylesbury butter and dairy-fed pork, apples, cabbages and cucumbers, alarming supplies of cats' meat, cart loads of water cresses, and we know not what else, for the daily consumption of the metropolis. No sooner do these disappear than at ten minutes' interval arrive other trains with Manchester packs and bales, Liverpool cotton, American provisions, Worcester gloves, Kidderminster carpets, Birmingham and Staffordshire hardware . . . At a later hour of the morning these are followed by other trains with the heaviest class of traffic, stones, bricks, iron girders, iron pipes, ale . . . coal, hay, straw, grain, flour and salt . . .'

(From *Railway News, 1864*)

The Importance of Railways

2. Railways were built, in the first instance, to move goods and people quickly and cheaply between two places. This was what the early planners and engineers intended.
Read Source B, which describes what railways were intended to achieve.
(a) Make a list of all the goods which were carried into London by the night trains.
(b) For *each* item you have written down, make a separate list of all the people who would have benefited from having had this particular item carried quickly and efficiently by the railways.
(c) Which people would not have benefited from having these goods carried by rail to London?

SOURCE C

Chambers' Journal was printed regularly and contained many informative and 'uplifting' articles. This is part of one about the changes which had happened as a result of the railways.

'The most important of these changes is the springing up of new towns. On the Birmingham railway, a station was made at Wolverton, about midway from London, the company erecting a refreshment room and a few sheds for their engines. Around these buildings a town has rapidly sprung up, and is so well populated, that the railway directors built a church.

Not the least important effect is the facilities they have afforded to the humbler classes for recreation. Short trips give the working classes the opportunity of seeing that which they would never have been able, under the stage-coach and wagon dynasty, to behold. The artisan, cooped up, and constantly breathing bad air, has now the opportunity, on every available holiday, of making excursions into the country.

A railway train takes masses of people of all ranks and conditions. The rich are brought into contact and converse with the poor. Nothing opens men's minds, so much as seeing a variety of things, of places, and of men. The greater the number of travellers, then, the greater the social improvement.'

(From *Chambers' Journal*, 21st September 1844)

SOURCE D

You read earlier how George and Robert Stephenson built over half of the British railway network. In 1856 Robert Stephenson made a speech to the Institute of Civil Engineers. This is part of what he said:

'. . . The results of railways were astounding. 90,000 men were employed directly and upwards of 40,000 collaterally [*indirectly*]; 130,000 men with their wives and families, representing a population of 500,000 souls; so that one in fifty of the entire population of the kingdom might be said to be dependent upon railways.'

(From Robert Stephenson, *Address to the Institution of Civil Engineers*, 1856)

3. Read Sources C and D.
These both describe some results of building railways which were not intended by the early planners and engineers.
(a) What unintended results are described in these sources?
(b) What other unintended results of railway building can you think of?
(c) Which do you consider to have been the more important, the intended or the unintended results of railway building?

SOURCE E

The Economist, a journal which was published regularly throughout the nineteenth century, contained articles on many topics. This is part of one which describes the benefits of railways:

'Now, who have specially benefitted by this vast invention?
The rich, whose horse and carriages carried them in comfort over the known world? – the middle classes, to whom stage coaches and mails were an accessible mode of conveyance? – or the poor, whom the cost of locomotion condemned often to an almost vegetable existence? Clearly the latter. The rail-road is the Magna Carta of their freedom. How few among the last generation ever stirred beyond their own village? How few among the present will die without visiting London? . . . The number who left Manchester by cheap trips in one week of holiday time last year exceeded 202,000; against 150,000 in 1849, and 116,000 in 1848.'

(From *The Economist*, 1851)

4. The author of Source E clearly believes that the poor benefited more from the railways than the rich and middle classes. Do you agree?
Remember to give as much evidence as possible to support your answer.

7

THE GREAT EXHIBITION

From First Ideas to Final Building

Manchester seemed to be empty in 1851! Clearly the cartoon on the right was an exaggeration, but Cruikshank was trying to make a point. A great many people had left Manchester. Where had they gone? Cruikshank himself supplied the answer in the cartoon below.

It was not only people from Manchester who had gone to London in 1851. Sometimes it must have seemed as if the whole world was there.

Two cartoons by George Cruikshank

MANCHESTER in 1851.

Planning

It was Prince Albert, Queen Victoria's husband, who had the idea of holding an international exhibition. A parliamentary commission was set up to investigate the possibilities. Eventually, it was decided that the exhibition could be held. It would display the work of all nations, not only Britain. What was more, it was to be organised by Prince Albert himself. It was to be called the 'Great Exhibition of the Works of Industry of all Nations'. Prince Albert told guests at a banquet:

'. . . the exhibition of 1851 is to give a true test and a living picture of the point of development at which the whole of mankind has arrived in this great task, and a new starting point from which all nations will be able to direct their further exertions. . .'

The problem, of course, was where to put this exhibition. The Building Committee, which included Isambard Kingdom Brunel and Robert Stephenson, decided to hold a competition. They believed that the building itself would be very important. Brunel hoped that it would be the most important exhibit of all:

'I believe that there is no one object to be exhibited so peculiarly fitted for competition as the design and construction of the vast building itself. Skill of construction, economy of construction and rapidity of construction would call forth all those resources for which England is distinguished . . .'

Many people tried their hand at designing a special hall for the Great Exhibition. All 245 designs which were submitted were rejected. Eventually, Joseph Paxton, who managed the Duke of Devonshire's vast estates, took matters in hand. He was more than just an estate manager; he was a highly successful businessman and a director of the Midland Railway. Furthermore, Paxton had been designing buildings for years, and had written an article about them in 1835 for the *Magazine for Botany*. Paxton's buildings, of course, were mainly conservatories, and were built from glass with an iron framework. He had recently finished a large conservatory at the Duke of Devonshire's family home, Chatsworth. This conservatory was designed specially to house an exotic South American water lily, named 'Victoria Regina'. The design which Paxton sent to the Building Committee was based upon his design for this special conservatory. It was huge: 1,848 feet long, 408 feet wide and 100 feet high at its highest point. It was built, of course, of glass with an iron framework, and was wonderfully light and airy. It could be built very quickly because it was pre-fabricated and the sections of iron and glass could be assembled elsewhere and only finally put together on the building site. It relied, too, on up-to-date technology. The interchangeable sections could not have been built without machine-tools to make sure that the sections were precision-built and would fit together. Plate-glass was needed in enormous quantities, and was supplied by Chance Brothers of Smethwick who had developed the necessary techniques and could guarantee delivery at the right time and at the right cost.

The Building Committee accepted Paxton's design without argument. Almost immediately the magazine *Punch* nicknamed it the 'Crystal Palace', even though several people, including the critic Leigh Hunt, pointed out that '. . . it was neither crystal nor a palace.'

Building

It was decided that the Crystal Palace should be built in Hyde Park, close to the centre of London. In August and September 1850, thirty-nine labourers levelled the site and laid drainage pipes. Then they began on the main building. No scaffolding was used – only blocks, pulleys, masts and ropes. Gradually the work-force of thirty-nine labourers was increased until over two thousand men were working on the site.

The 'Palace' was put up at incredible speed. This was due, partly, to the large work-force. It was also due to the way in which this work-force was organised, and to the fact that large sections of the 'Palace' were built elsewhere and only put together on site. Machines were brought to the site which could cut gutters and window frames to the correct length and size. Teams of glaziers (men who put glass into windows) worked in hammocks slung under the iron framework. By working as a team, sliding glass panels into place, it was possible for 80 men to fix over 18,000 panes of glass in a week. 1,060 iron columns were put up, supporting 2,224 trellis girders and 353 trusses. Thirty miles of guttering was used, together with 600,000 cubic feet of timber. Early in December the great semicircular roof-ribs were ready to be hoisted into position:

Queen Victoria and Prince Albert arriving at the opening of the Great Exhibition, May 1 1851

You will see from this picture that the Crystal Palace was large enough to have fully grown trees inside! These all added to the feeling of light, air and space.

People were very interested in the building works. Crowds gathered each day to watch what was happening. Indeed, on one day at the end of February it was reckoned that over 100,000 people were watching progress. The contractors decide to charge 5s for admission to the site. This way people could watch what was going on, and the money they contributed was put into a workmen's accident fund.

Finally work was finished – and on time. The whole building operation had taken about nine months. A magnificent Crystal Palace stood in Hyde Park, ready to house the Great Exhibition.

1st May 1851

This is how the journalist Henry Mayhew described London on the morning of 1st May 1851:

'. . . With the first gleam of daylight, the boys of London had taken up their places in the trees . . . men and women grouped round the rails, determined at least to have a good place for seeing the opening of the World's Show . . . Some were pouring in at the Park gates, laden with tables and chairs for the sight-seers to stand upon. Others

came with the omnipresent street provisions – huge trucks filled with bottles of ginger beer – baskets of gingerbread and 'fatty cakes' – and tins of brandyballs and hardbakes – while from every quarter there streamed girls and women with round wicker sieves piled up in pyramids with oranges . . . as the morning advanced the crowds . . . grew denser and denser . . . fathers with their wives and children, skipping jauntily along, and youths with their gaily dressed sweethearts, in lively coloured shawls and ribbons . . . All London, and half the country, and a good part of the world, were wending their way to see the Queen pass in state to open the GREAT EXHIBITION OF ALL NATIONS.'

The Opening Ceremony

The boys who had climbed the trees, and the men, women and children lining the streets and filling Hyde Park, had watched well over a thousand official state carriages pass through the gates of Hyde Park that morning. They carried important people who held official positions in Great Britain and abroad. They carried, too, the rich and the famous who had been specially invited to watch the opening ceremony. By 2 o'clock over 30,000 guests were waiting inside the Crystal Palace for Queen Victoria to arrive and officially open the Great Exhibition.

The Queen wrote, later, in her Journal:

'. . . The park presented a wonderful spectacle, crowds streaming through it . . . The day was bright and all bustle and excitement . . . A little rain fell, just as we started, but before we reached the Crystal Palace, the sun shone and gleamed upon the gigantic edifice [*building*], upon which the flags of every nation were flying . . . The tremendous cheering, the joy expressed in every face, the vastness of the building, with all its decorations and exhibits . . . all this was indeed moving, and a day to live for ever.'

The Exhibition and the Exhibits

At a very early stage in planning the Great Exhibition, it was decided that:

'. . . the whole space of any building should be equally divided, and that one half should be offered to Foreign countries, and the other reserved to Great Britain and her colonies . . .'

Exhibits had poured in from all over the world. They were accepted under six major headings: raw materials; machinery; manufactures – textile fabrics; manufactures – metallic, vitreous and ceramic; fine arts; and miscellaneous, which covered everything the other headings did not. Each heading was sub-divided, and no less than thirty 'sub-classes' of exhibits were formed in this way. Over 100,000 items of all shapes, sizes, importance and interest were sent in by 5,000 exhibitors. All the exhibits were carefully displayed in their correct hall or gallery.

There was a tremendous emphasis on power and technology. At the approach to the Exhibition there was a huge block of coal weighing twenty-four tons; enormous ornate cast-iron gates made at Coalbrookdale stood inside. At the front of the Machinery Court stood the powerful hydraulic press which was used to raise the giant tubes needed for the Britannia Bridge, which had been designed by Robert Stephenson.

The official Exhibition commentator described what was happening elsewhere in the Machinery Court:

'On every side, around this Stephenson apparatus, thousands of little machines, which well deserved the epithet [*name*] of beautiful, were hard at work, and ingeniously occupied in the manufacture of all sorts of useful articles from knife handles to envelopes . . .'

Naysmith's steam-hammer was there, along with spinning and weaving machines, steam engines of every description, and steam locomotives. There, too, were

The Inauguration: Queen Victoria announces the Great Exhibition open

precision tools from the workshops of Maudslay and Whitworth. Together, the whole Machinery Court demonstrated a combination of power and precision which had turned Britain into the 'workshop of the world'.

Machines did not only make useful articles. As they became more and more specialised, machines could be made to produce all kinds of effects which hand-craftsmen could not manage. For example, ordinary household objects like teapots and vases, could be made highly ornamental. New materials could be mass-produced: papier mâché, for instance, could be moulded into elaborate shapes. Materials were adapted freely, and so were designs. Wallpapers were printed with exotic designs of flowers and fruit; carpets woven with intricate deeply coloured patterns on them. If a machine could do it, it would be done, regardless of commonsense or taste!

When William Morris (1834–96), who was to become a designer, artist and writer, visited the Great Exhibition, he refused to go round to look at the exhibits. He said it was all 'wonderfully ugly'. Others, like William Whitely, were so inspired that they began to plan large shops with vast plate-glass windows.

There were some indications that Britain's supremacy in industry and technology would be challenged. Many people were particularly interested in the American exhibits. *The Times* newspaper praised the 'useful character of the display' and the 'several very interesting machines'. Among these were McCormick's reaping machine which speeded up and completely mechanised reaping; a sewing machine which could be worked by one person and could produce 600 stitches a minute; a prize-winning lock which was better than the best Britain could produce; a wide range of Colt revolvers made from parts which could be interchanged; and an ice-making machine.

However, the Great Exhibition clearly demonstrated to all those who visited it that Britain was, in 1851, the supreme nation as far as technology was concerned. The Great Exhibition catalogue, along with advertisements for Colman's mustard and Dinneford's mag-nesia, carried advertisements for two books. These were *The Progress of the Nation* by G.R. Porter and J.R. M'Culloch's book *A Descriptive and Statistical Account of the British Empire*. These two books, published towards the end of the 1830s by John Murray and Longman respectively, were among the first to use statistics to demonstrate Britain's industrial progress.

One of the most important themes of the Great Exhibition was summed up in one of the Exhibition's mottoes printed in the catalogue:

'The progress of the human race, resulting from the common labour of all men, ought to be the final object of the exertion [*work*] of each individual. In promoting this end, we are carrying out the will of the great and blessed God.'

The Visitors

They came pouring into the Great Exhibition – rich and poor – in carriages and on foot. Some were brought to London by special excursion trains; some rented great houses close by and stayed there for weeks with their servants and families. It was the event of the year – if not the decade – and whether you were a society duchess or a draper from Rotherham, you had to be there.

Season Tickets

The rich and well-to-do bought season tickets, and visited the exhibition often. That way they could wander through the halls and galleries as they wished, and spend time looking at the exhibits which particularly interested them. Prince Albert was issued with the very first season ticket to the Great Exhibition.

Some, however, had doubts about the general safety of the whole enterprise. Lady Charlotte Guest wrote in her diary:

This drawing by Cruikshank shows the popularity of the Great Exhibition

April 30th
A large and pleasant party at Lady John Russell's.
Everybody was talking of tomorrow's opening.
Most people were going . . . Some days before, a
great deal had been said about the dangers
attendant on the ceremony. Some affirmed that
the whole edifice would tumble down, some that
the noise of the cannons would shatter the glass,
many that the crowd and rush at the door would
be intolerable, and not a few expected that riots
and rebellions and conspiracies were suddenly to
break out . . .'

Nothing of the kind happened, of course. Everyone
was able to walk in perfect safety around the Crystal
Palace. Indeed, the Queen and the royal children made
one of the first ever royal 'walk-abouts'. They mingled
with the crowds, attended only by a handful of constables with long sticks.

Five Shilling and One Shilling Days

The organisers wanted as many people as possible to
visit the Great Exhibition. So that shopkeepers and
seamstresses, miners and ladies' maids, factory operatives and crossing sweepers could all afford the entry
charges, a sliding scale was used. Each day of the week
had a different charge for entry. On some days the
charge was £1, which was the most anyone could pay
for a day's admission. Then there were:

'. . . the five shilling Saturday people, the half
crown Friday people, and the great bulk . . . in
somewhat humbler circumstances, who congregate
on the shilling days . . .'

There were, of course, people who were too poor to be
able to afford the shilling entry fee. The organisers
were totally opposed to making a 'free' day, and so
the richer members of the community took matters
into their own hands:

'Clergymen and landed proprietors in remote rural
districts have organised plans by which whole
troops of agricultural labourers, with their wives
and children, have been enabled to visit London
once in their lives, and to see the marvels of art,
skill and industry congregated together in a
building so novel in its construction, and so
imposing in appearance . . . Manufacturers in the
provincial towns . . . have not only given their
workpeople a holiday to enable them to visit the
Exhibition, but have in numerous instances paid
the expenses both of the trip and of their
admission . . . bankers, solicitors and others have
remembered the services of their clerks and
employees, and afforded them both time and the
means to partake in the general jubilee . . .'

Even the emigration committees (see pages 107–8)
made sure that those who were leaving for ever to
begin a new life elsewhere saw the Great Exhibition:

'Parties of humble emigrants have come to Hyde
Park, in order that they might not take their last

THE POUND AND THE SHILLING.
"Whoever Thought of Meeting You Here?"

A cartoon from Punch 1851

look of England without seeing the wondrous
Exhibition; and their expenses have been paid by
the philanthropic [*caring*] individuals by whose
assistance [*help*] they were able to leave the old
world for the new . . .'

By having different entry charges on different days, the
organisers of the Great Exhibition were making it possible for the rich and the poor never to meet. Some historians have suggested that this was what they
intended. However, matters clearly didn't work out
like that. Queen Victoria visited the Great Exhibition
often, and several times made a point of going on
'shilling' days when poorer people would be there.
Why do you think she did this?

The Effects of the Exhibition

Clearly the Great Exhibition was a success. It was
visited by over 6 million people. They ate 2 million
buns whilst they were doing so, and drank a million
bottles of mineral water. (Beer was not allowed inside
the Crystal Palace). Clearly, however, many millions
must have gone hungry, brought a packed lunch, or
bought food elsewhere!

One of the important things which the Great Exhibition did for Britain was, as you have seen, to show
the whole world how superior Great Britain was in the

many industries which it had been the first to develop. Yet it did more than this. The Great Exhibition brought about a change in attitudes. The organisers and the respectable middle classes were surprised to see that the respectable working-class families from the midlands and north did not vandalise the palace or the exhibits. There was no violence. Indeed, the extra policemen who had been called in on the 'shilling' days were not needed. The only real problem was the orange peel which was found at the bottom of some of the fountains!

The excursion trains, which the railway companies had put on specially, had proved very popular. Afterwards the companies ran more and more excursion trains to more and more seaside resorts and inland towns and cities of interest. They would also put on an 'excursion special' for a specific event if they thought that sufficient people wanted to go to see it.

Yet amid all the celebrations and self congratulations, there was a darker side. In April 1850 the cartoon below was published in the magazine *Punch*. It shows 'Mr. Punch' displaying his imaginary exhibition: an industrious needlewoman, a seventy-five-year-old labourer, a distressed shoemaker, and a worker in the 'sweated' industries. These people, and thousands like them, the cartoon is saying, have not benefited from the industrial prosperity of Britain which will be celebrated by the Great Exhibition of 1851.

SPECIMENS FROM MR. PUNCH'S INDUSTRIAL EXHIBITION OF 1850

(TO BE IMPROVED IN 1851).

INDEX

Page numbers in bold type are references to pictures